Heretical Leadership

How to avoid Square Wheel Management

HERETICAL LEADERSHIP

How to avoid
SQUARE WHEEL MANAGEMENT

Barry Jackson

ecademyPRESS
www.ecademy-press.com

Heretical Leadership
How to avoid Square Wheel Management

First published in 2011 by
Ecademy Press
48 St Vincent Drive, St Albans, Herts, AL1 5SJ
info@ecademy-press.com
www.ecademy-press.com

Printed and bound by Lightning Source in the UK and USA
Designed by Michael Inns
Artwork by Karen Gladwell

Printed on acid-free paper from managed forests. This book is printed on demand, so no copies will be remaindered or pulped.

ISBN 978-1-907722-53-0

Contents

Introduction

Most people look at what everyone else is doing and think to themselves, 'if that's what everyone else is doing, it must be the best way.' Indeed, there are times when I think business leaders would fit square tyres to their company cars if they discovered that their competitors thought it was a good idea. One of the things you need to get to grips with, and quickly, is that so many things are clearly not working that it's time to lead some of the most sacred of cows to where they belong: the slaughterhouse.

One thing we must not do is confuse a heretic with an entrepreneur (though it's possible to be both) or a maverick. An entrepreneur blazes trails where no trails existed before. An entrepreneur has the courage to try new things and is not afraid of taking risks. An entrepreneur also focuses on an improved outcome. The minute he sees that his new approach is taking him further from that goal, he has the humility to admit that it's not working and experiments until he finds what does. A maverick believes in change for its own sake. A maverick clings resolutely to ideology; very politically correct a maverick is. Mavericks pursue the things they would **like to work**, long after it's been proven that they don't. A maverick feels uncomfortable when challenged.

So, if a heretic is neither of these things, what is a heretic? A heretic is all in favour of new ideas, as long as they produce progress. When they are adopted *in favour of what was previously working well* and the situation is going from bad to worse, a heretic challenges the very beliefs and values which produce this result.

Heretics tell it the way it is. Heretics are the scourge of political correctness. Heretics have never been popular; they may end up being burned at the stake. By the time you've finished reading this, you're either going to love me or hate me. The fact is that political correctness is as rife in business as it is any other walk of life.

One or two simple examples will illustrate my point. I'm appealing to your own experience here and for a very good reason. If I tell you anything which is contrary to what you have experienced yourself, be very suspicious of what you're being told; it's probably wrong. Take a look at the jobs page in any newspaper: have a look at how many employers claim to pride themselves on excellent customer service. They all do. No one ever says: 'I don't give a stuff about the image we project to our customers.' No; but they say it in the way they behave. Am I the only one who tries to ring a firm or a school or a hospital only to hear a robotic voice which says something like this?

'If you want to speak to the quantum physics department, please press one. If you want to speak to our resident falconer, please press two. If you are considering legal proceedings against us, please press three.' And so it goes on. Recently, having made my choice, I then got the final insult: 'All our lines are busy at present. Your call is important to us, please hold.' Don't **tell me** how important my call is to you. I can tell when my call is important. How? I get through to a real live human being at the very first attempt. That's how I can tell. In a recent survey, the multiple-option voice message was way up there in the nation's list of pet hates. If we care so much about excellent customer service, why do so many establishments persist with something they know provokes rage in every caller they get? The answer is that they **don't** care. They don't give a stuff!

Let's look at a second example. Go back to the jobs page again. This time, however, look at the qualities required of candidates. How many include 'excellent communication skills'? My guestimate: a third, at least.

Or how about this? Has this ever happened to you, or am I the only one? You phone someone's personal mobile, personal extension or direct line number and you hear the following message:

'Sorry I wasn't able to take your call right now. Please leave a message after the tone and I'll get back to you as soon as possible.'

Makes your call sound really important doesn't' it? I'm appealing to your personal experience again. When you hear that message, how confident are you that you **will** ever receive a call back? What does 'as soon as possible' mean, anyway? Here's what that voice message nearly always means, in my experience (maybe yours is different):

'Please leave a message after the tone. I may return your call, but unless I already know you, don't put money on it, because I probably won't.'

I have heard that message, almost word for word, time after time after time after time after time... The conclusions I have come to are these:

▼ At least 30 million people in the UK are using the same voice mail message.

▼ Of those, 29.9 million (possibly an underestimate) have no intention of responding to most of their callers.

▼ At least 30 million people have about as much creative thought as a beetle.

▼ Of those, 29.9 million break their word several times, quite deliberately, on a daily basis.

This is not complicated stuff. How long does it take to record a unique message, update it each day and keep your word? If you can't do that much for your callers, what right do you have to claim that you pride yourself on being an excellent communicator? What right do you have to expect it of your staff if you won't role model something as basic as that? That's not excellence; it's worse than mediocre.

It's time we asked ourselves some serious questions and started acting on what we **knew** was the truth even before we asked the question.

▼ If the standard of leadership is so high, why is it that one-third of all sick days are put down to stress, costing the economy 13.5 million working days a year?

▼ If team building is such a good idea, why is staff turnover higher than at any time in living memory?

▼ If the standard of leadership is so high, why is it that so many staff need counselling?

▼ Most staff do not need counselling. They need a sense of community, a sense of belonging.

▼ If team building is so effective, why are there so many courses on conflict management?

▼ Courses in personality profiling and neurolinguistic programming abound, but if basic communication skills are lacking, it's like teaching calculus to someone who can't add up.

▼ The people we refer to as demotivated are not demotivated; they're lacking inspiration.

▼ The purpose of setting targets is not to intimidate, threaten and manipulate people. If that becomes their purpose, the result will be demoralization.

▼ There is a world of difference between heroes and mere winners.

The guidance provided in these pages is as relevant in family and non-profit-making situations as it is in business, because the principles are the same. That's why what I share is based on my observations of successful sales teams, successful marriages, successful sports teams and harmonious congregations. It's based on my observations of how, sooner or later, things fall apart when these principles are ignored. They work equally well with adults and with children. And they work equally well whether the organization is commercial or voluntary.

Before you can become a good leader, you have to experience being *led* by an excellent leader. This book will help you recognize a first-rate leader when you find one. It will help you distinguish between the truly inspiring leader and the mere 'boss' who's attended every known course on leadership principles so he can exhibit the Investors In People plaque in the company reception area, but who pays mere lip service to the principles he learned. When you do find a true leader, ask yourself what principles this leader lives by and role model your leadership on this person. Go one stage further: **ask permission to adopt him or her as your leadership mentor.** It's the greatest compliment you could offer anyone and no leader is going to refuse.

If you find my approach controversial, it's meant to be. My belief is that personal integrity is what makes us worthy of success, at home, in our communities and at work. Those of us who support the values expressed here can, by our example, prove that huge success and personal integrity are not only compatible. but that, without integrity, lasting success is highly unlikely.

If you don't agree, burn me at the stake
and serve me medium rare!

CHAPTER ONE

Heretical Leadership

A few weeks ago, while I had half an hour to spare, I wandered into a car showroom. There it was, my dream car, a Jaguar XKR convertible. It was black, it was sleek, it had alloy wheels and it had white leather seats. But it wasn't like those loud Italian jobs that scream at you to get your attention. This car had no need to do that. This car had class; £78,000 worth of class, and it was worth every penny – if you had £78,000 of spare cash lying around, that is.

What gives a leader class?

What is it that gives a leader class? What is it that distinguishes a leader from a manager and makes that person a role model to the whole team, a person the whole team looks up to as their personal hero? Let me share three stories with you. In each case I have protected the identities of the people concerned by changing their names and I have altered the stories slightly for the same reason. In all but the very fine detail, all three stories are absolutely true.

Colin was one of those rather eccentric, geeky guys that you meet in research departments. He had no dress sense whatsoever and even when wearing a suit he managed to look shabby. But Colin was a character and was extremely popular with all his colleagues. He was also a devoted family man; his two children were his pride and joy and he carried pictures of them everywhere. One morning, at breakfast, the kids were bickering; you know the sort of thing. The two parents were getting irritated: 'Stop it you two. Get a move on. You're going to be late for school.' As they set off, the little girl suddenly realized that she hadn't given daddy a hug. She never left without giving daddy a hug. She ran back and threw herself into his arms.

'You're the best daddy in all the world,' she said. 'I love you very much. I always will.'

'I love you too, Little Princess,' Colin said. 'I love you with all my heart.'

She was late and afraid she might get into trouble. She ran out of the door, there was a screech of tyres and a bang. Even as he ran from the house, Colin knew that his little princess had been taken from him forever.

What's this got to do with leadership? Let me tell you. The day after the tragedy happened, George, the sales manager, sent a memo to the entire team. Here's what it said: 'On the day of the funeral, the company will be closed for business as a mark of respect to Colin and his family. If you live too far away to make it to the funeral, I want you to finish work early. I want you to be at the school gates when your kids come out, and I want you to tell them that you cherish them.'

Now here's a question for you: how many sales managers would have done what George did for his team? Very few. Very few indeed. But something happened that day. Everyone in George's team knew that he would have done the same for any one of them and it made no difference what their level of performance was at the time. George's love for them, as people, was unconditional. George didn't know it at the time, but the spirit that was birthed by that simple, but powerful act of love for his team was to save the company in a way that he would never have predicted.

Now for the second story. Janice was a dedicated member of the sales team. She worked extremely hard but her sales target was an ambitious one and, with just a few weeks to go to the end of the year, she was running just short of 98 per cent of her target. The news that her best friend had been killed in a car crash devastated Janice. Naturally, she wanted time off to attend the funeral. Had it been a family member who had been killed, UK law would have entitled her to take compassionate leave. But it wasn't. And since it was November, she had already used up her annual leave. She requested a day's unpaid leave. Her request was refused on the grounds that there was no legal entitlement and her first priority was to hit her sales target. Incensed, Janice took the day off anyway and announced that she would be looking for another job with immediate effect. Come February, she was working for a competitor. So were half her colleagues. They left before their manager had a chance to treat them the same way. Did the company hit its sales target that year? Well actually, yes it did; but the following year...

Now for the last story and it concerns, once more, that first sales manager, George. About two years after the tragedy involving Colin's little girl, the company suffered a serious problem on their production line. The problem didn't look like being solved any time soon. Stock began to run low and it looked as if some of their best customers would have to take their business to the competition. George called his team together for a crisis meeting. There would, he announced, be no Christmas bonus that year or bonuses of any kind; neither would there be any salary reviews because the company couldn't afford it. He could not, he told the team, guarantee everyone's job for very much longer. 'Most of you have families and all of you have mortgages,' he said. 'If anyone feels that, in the interests of family security, they must seek alternative employment, I will not stand in the way.' No high fives at that meeting, then! But not one person left that sales team. Not one.

You see, George had class.

Did the company hit its sales target that year? Nowhere near. But the following year? You want to know about the following year? That was the year they broke all records, and the first of the best five years in the company's history. It was the year they all went quad biking in the pouring rain and got really, really filthy. I know. I was there!

When George looked at the world, he looked at it with straight eyes, with clean hands and without shame. George was no mere manager; George was a leader who cherished every single member of his team. They knew it too, and they wouldn't have left his team if you'd offered them a fortune.

You don't know how good a team you have until you face a crisis together. Have you ever watched one of those remarkable matches where a football team is three goals down at half-time and they end up winning 4:3? Have you ever watched a match at Wimbledon where a player is two sets down, survives three match points and goes on to win. Why does the whole world get behind people like that? You don't need me to answer that question do you? We all admire guts. We all admire the team or individual who comes back from a hopeless position. We see a display of real character and we admire it. So what if someone hasn't hit their target? Does that make her a loser? Or does it simply mean she hasn't won – yet?

> *What should our reaction be to one of our team who simply hasn't won — yet?*
>
> *The usual response, in most companies, is to look for ways to 'manage him out.'*

CHAPTER TWO

The Heresy of Goal Setting

Now then, before you throw up your hands in horror, let me say right from the outset that goal setting in business, education and personal life is essential if any progress is going to be made. Even I am not so heretical as to suggest that goal setting is a bad idea.

A very good friend of ours told us recently that she is trying to lose weight. That seems to have been her goal for as long as we can remember. We have known her for well over 20 years and she appears to us to be exactly the same shape she has always been. I've never had the heart to ask her the obvious questions: 'What weight were you at the beginning of last month and what was your target weight for the beginning of this month?'

I'm sure she has never asked herself the second of those two questions. So, before we go any further, let's agree that losing weight is not a goal. Losing three pounds in the next month is a goal. It's a SMART goal – Specific, Measurable, Attainable, Realistic and Timely.

So where's the heresy? Here comes a clue. I have recently heard sales people say it of their sales managers and I've heard teachers say it of Ofsted (Office for Standards in Education) inspectors: 'No matter what I achieve, they just keep raising the bar. I get that *pressurized feeling* that nothing is ever going to be good enough. The bar will just be raised higher and higher so I'm *bound to fail eventually.* That will give them an excuse to say I'm incompetent.'

One in three days lost to sickness is due to stress. And what causes stress in the work place? Stress occurs when the demands of the job exceed a person's perceived ability or willingness to perform. We've got to get away from the idea that failure to hit a goal is always the same thing as underachievement (though it may be).

What makes a good or bad goal?

It's not that goal setting is wrong or irrelevant; it's not. But let's examine what makes a good or a bad goal and, as an example, let's say that I place a bow and some arrows in your hand, lead you into a field and say, 'Okay, let's see how good you are at archery.' Your first question is going to be, 'Where's the target? What am I aiming at?' Without a target, the exercise is pretty pointless.

Let's say you're a complete beginner. What's a *realistic* goal for you? Unless I'm a pretty heartless coach, I'm going to place the target quite close and I'm going to encourage you if you hit any part of it. Even this might prove a challenge! However, as you improve you will reach the stage where you're hitting the target almost every time. It's time to make it a bit more difficult. If this is not done, there's no longer a *challenge* and there's no *satisfaction* in hitting it. But it must still be *realistic.*

> ▼ Without challenge, there's no inspiration.

> ▼ Without satisfaction, there's no reward for effort.

> ▼ Without realism, challenge becomes a threat.

Without all three elements, you will give up, either out of boredom or because you feel set up for failure and criticism.

'A mountain half the size will only make you half the climber.'

Todd Skinner.

'If you don't stand at the base of the mountain, unsure of whether you can reach the summit, then the mountain is not worthy of your best efforts. To be worthy of your best efforts, the mountain should appear intimidating.'

Todd Skinner.

In the case of archery, there are two ways I can make the shot more challenging. One is to move the target further and further away; the other is to reduce the size of the area that counts. The whole target is no longer good enough; you need a bull's eye. So far so good; but if I increase the distance indefinitely, I will eventually place the target beyond the range of the bow! To expect you to hit the target now is clearly unreasonable, however good an archer you are. The goal I've set you is no longer exciting, it's threatening and you're going to get disheartened and disillusioned. If the target is beyond the range of the bow, I'm not going to change that by offering you a huge incentive for hitting it!

Your team is not going to chase any incentive if the goal seems beyond their reach. If your team feels they are being set goals that are beyond their reach, they will feel manipulated. They are probably right!

So what makes a good goal?

Before I suggest an answer, let me share a short story. Not long before I left the pharmaceutical industry, I was in conversation with one of the UK's leading experts on MRSA control. He showed me the government targets for reducing the incidence of hospital MRSA infection. He followed this with the words I have heard so often in hospitals, industry and schools: 'It's all very well setting these targets but no one tells us how, exactly, we're supposed to deliver a result like this. Believe me Barry, no one would be more delighted than I if I felt there was any chance of achieving it. But we're not going to; it's not going to happen.' The golden rule of goal setting that's most frequently violated is that the powers that be, and that could be you, must **get agreement as to what is realistic from those whose job it is to deliver.** If they can't see any way of achieving it, they are probably right and their opinion is worth listening to. The problem comes when *you say it is* and *your team says it's not!* Now what do you do? Well, in my experience, it's not as difficult as it may sound because there's usually room for manoeuvre – quite a bit of room *if you approach it correctly. But you must leave yourself room for manoeuvre.*

We could, of course, set a goal that's almost impossible to miss! We could place the target just a few feet away so you could hit it with your eyes closed. If a goal is 100 per cent certain to be met, it wasn't challenging enough. That might be realistic, but if there's no challenge in hitting it there will be no satisfaction in hitting it either. What we want to do is set the distance so that both of us feel that you have an 80 to 95 per cent chance of hitting it. The point is that between 80 and 95 per cent there's quite a bit of leeway and room for negotiation as to what's reasonable. *Leaving yourself room for manoeuvre will make you appear extremely fair and reasonable, which is critical in maintaining team loyalty.* If you both agree that the goal is a challenging one and that hitting it is not a certainty, any threat of failing to deliver is removed! In fact, a 95 per cent achievement becomes a success. You will now find that you will get buy in rather than resistance from your team, because failure to hit 100 per cent of target is no longer synonymous with underperformance.

The problems with goal setting

In my experience, the problems with goal setting are caused by one or more of the following:

▼ Setting the corporate goal before consulting 'the troops'. For example, it's going to be very difficult to convince your team that a corporate goal to achieve £1m sales in 12 months is realistic if you have 10 sales people and the turnover of the highest achiever is £50k!

▼ Loading the highest increase onto the highest achiever. This is a terribly easy mistake to make. Not only does your best team member feel you're taking advantage, but the gap between the highest and lowest achiever is widened even if the target is hit, and the organization is heading towards the 'eggs in one basket' situation.

▼ Setting goals which are mutually exclusive. For example, a telephone call centre recently set a goal for staff to make 10 outgoing calls per hour (average time on the phone was five minutes) and to receive a minimum of 10 incoming calls per hour (average time on the phone was three minutes). No wonder the staff felt they were in for a rollicking whatever they did. They were; and most of them left. Now there's a surprise!

▼ Setting tasks and goals which seriously interfere with a team member's private life. Would you be surprised to know that 86 per cent of British managers say the demands of their jobs pose a serious threat to their family relationships?

▼ A goal does not become realistic simply by telling a team member that it's just *got to be achieved.*

▼ A goal does not become realistic by saying, 'If you're not willing to do it, I'll find someone who is.'

▼ A goal does not become realistic simply by offering a huge incentive for achieving it!

These are insensitive, crude and cowardly forms of management. Lack of respect, in any form, is threatening. If a teacher talked down to you when you were at school, how did you feel? What was your reaction? How did your parents react when you told them how you had been spoken to? So, if it's not okay to talk to a child like that, at what age does it suddenly become okay to talk down to people? At what level of seniority does it no longer matter to a person to receive praise and encouragement? Could it be when someone becomes head of department? Head teacher? Managing director? The answer is that it never ceases to matter. So, on your way up, don't give encouragement only to people lower in the pecking order to you. Be encouraging to people above you in the organization as well. They're probably starved of praise more than any other people in the building. Isn't that just sucking up, though? It certainly can be; but if you know when the encouragement is genuine, so will the person receiving your praise; and that applies wherever they are in the hierarchy. Also, never forget that if the need arises to challenge the position of more senior colleagues they are far more likely to take it in the spirit you intended when they know that you regularly say good things about them. If you only comment on their decisions and policies when you're unhappy about them, you just come across as whingeing.

Finally, I think we all too often make the mistake of confusing high expectation with high demand; they are not the same animal. 'I want that report ready and on my desk by 4.30 p.m. Understood?' That's a demand. I don't know about you, but my gut reaction to that kind of demand is, 'Just who do you think you're talking to? Don't you talk to me like that.' On the other hand, how would you feel if someone said to you, 'Of course, I don't expect much of you, really?' How about hurt, angry and disappointed? I would. We like people to have a high expectation of us. We are inspired by a high expectation that gives us something to live up to; something of which we can feel proud when we do. There are two lethal combinations when it comes to goal setting:

1. High encouragement/low expectation
2. High demand/unreasonable expectation

Remember this:

People may forget what you tell them.
They will never forget how you made
them feel.

CHAPTER THREE

Incentives are Heresy

Yes, you heard right. I did say forget incentives. There's a great line in the film Cool Runnings. The Jamaican bobsleigh team has lost belief that they can win the gold medal. Training is not going to plan, morale is low, and they're wondering if it's worth carrying on. After all, whoever heard of a Jamaican bobsleigh team? Here's what the coach says to lift his team: 'The gold medal is a wonderful thing; but if you're not enough without it, you're never going to be enough with it.'

The gold medal is the reward, but *if it's only an incentive, it will never measure up.* In that sense, incentives are a bit of an insult. The assumption behind offering incentives is that, without them, people will not be motivated; which is the same thing as saying they are uninspired. If that is so, there's a much more fundamental problem that needs to be addressed, and it's not going to be fixed by offering incentives.

Inspiration rarely responds to incentives

What all leaders want are inspired followers. Inspiration, however, rarely responds to incentives. In fact, truly heroic behaviour frequently occurs when there is not only no incentive at all, but serious self-sacrifice! How does that work? What produces inspiration? How do we recognize it? We may find it hard to put it into words, but recognize it we do. Think of the firefighters who went into the Twin Towers when it was obvious they were about to collapse. What inspired them to put their very lives at risk? Was it an incentive? Did someone offer them an expenses-paid week in the Bahamas if they went in? Was that why we admired them so much? When they were interviewed after the event and they were asked, 'What gave you the courage to go into a situation like that?' How many said it was the promise of a week in Hawaii or the opportunity to appear on TV? Suppose that *had* been their answer, what would *you* have thought of them? It's not incentives that inspir*e*, but *the cause* that inspires; the leader who believes in that cause; the leader who believes in you before you believe in yourself; the leader who encourages you. **Those who are not encouraging you have forfeited the right to influence you.**

If you know anything at all about English football, you must have heard of that legendary former manager of Liverpool, Bill Shankley. If you're reading this and you're an American, think of a man like Vince Lombardi. Bill was a man in that mould. It's hard to believe, today, that Liverpool have not always been in the top flight and that they have not always been a Premier Division side.

Back in the days when Liverpool's vision was to join that elite, a young and very talented defender called Ron Yeats was playing for a not-very-important team in Dundee. He had been spotted by one of Shankley's talent scouts and invited down to Anfield to meet Mr. Shankley, with a view to recruiting him into the Liverpool team. Shankley, however, had a challenge on his hands. Liverpool wasn't the only team trying to entice Ron Yeats to leave Dundee. Teams like Arsenal, Spurs and Manchester United had their eyes on him too; and they had the money to offer him a much more lucrative contract than Shankley could. In any case, why would the lad choose to join Liverpool when the opportunity was there to join one of the big three? Apparently, Ron Yeats asked that very question of Bill Shankley: 'Why would I want to join Liverpool when you're not even a Premier Division side?' Just listen to Shankley's reply: 'Right now, lad, we're not a Premier Division team, but we will be with *you* in the side.' To the dismay of the other bidders, Yeats turned down offers from all three and joined Liverpool. He went on to captain the team during Liverpool's glory years – as well as his country, Scotland.

Notice what Shankley did when he said to Yeats, 'We're not a Premier Division side, but we will be with you in the side.' He wasn't trying to convince Yeats that Liverpool was a better side. They weren't. Instead, he shared his vision for where he wanted to take Liverpool and his conviction that Yeats was the man to help him achieve that vision. He inspired Yeats to see himself as part of that vision, to see his new boss as a man who believed in him more than anyone else had ever done. Shankley saw all his players in that light; and I don't think Liverpool ever had a lower turnover of players. No one who played under Bill Shankley's leadership ever wanted to play for anyone else. Other teams thought it was about incentives. Shankley knew it was about vision. Shankley offered Yeats a cause.

I also think that we have a very narrow view of what it takes to inspire people. Most managers seem to think in terms of a monetary bonus, or just going out and having fun. Among the most effective ways to generate loyalty and to *really* make your people feel valued is to spring surprises on them. Reward them in ways they are simply not expecting. If you receive a message from your boss that he wants to see you in his office before you go home, what's the first thing that goes through your head? Your instinctive reaction is that you're in trouble, right? Why? Because that is usually what it means. So, how about creating a tradition, in your team, where a call to your office is a call to be looked forward to. How would it be if, every time you sent for someone, she would be saying to her colleagues, 'Guess what? I've been invited to the office before I go home,' and she says it with a great big smile of anticipation on her face because it usually means a reward. She just doesn't know what the reward is, that's all.

How to reward your team

There are dozens of ways you can reward your team and the rewards don't have to be huge. Let's suppose Valentine's day is coming up. How about calling someone to your office and saying something like this: 'Where are you taking Julie for Valentine's?' How would you like to take her to a really prestigious place? Where would she like to go more than any other place? How much extra will it take to make that possible?" And you give him the money. Someone's wedding anniversary might be approached in a similar way. For many people, an extra day off might be appreciated more than money. Let's say one of your team has performed exceptionally well, or worked a lot of extra hours without being asked to do so. How about taking her to one side on Friday afternoon and telling her you can manage without her 'til Tuesday; tell her to have a long weekend. If there's a person who's devoted to his children, why not buy a family ticket to Drayton Manor Theme Park or Alton Towers. Make the reward as personal as you can by making a note of anything you overhear in conversation that tells you what their favourite wine is, the football team they support, the restaurant at which they most enjoy eating out, their favourite hobby or pastime, or the shop where they most enjoy buying clothes.

One of the most inspiring managers I knew was a man who ran a small local company employing largely unskilled women, most of whom had young families and many of whom were single mothers. Clive (not his real name) realized that for these women the conflicting emotions involved in holding down a job and being a devoted mother could be stressful. Here's how he turned that challenge into inspiration. Firstly, he did not simply give them challenging performance targets; he encouraged them to do their jobs as efficiently as possible. He rewarded them by telling them that there would be no set working hours. They would work whatever hours were needed to complete the job. He also told them that if they completed their work early they could leave early. As a result, they were always looking for imaginative ways to work more efficiently and it was not unusual for them to be home with their children by 3.30.p.m. This not only gave them the opportunity to spend more time with their children, but it reduced the amount of money they spent on childminders. He also took the most unusual step of telling them all that he expected them to put their responsibilities as mothers ahead of their responsibilities as his employees. He told them that if one of their children was ill he expected them to stay at home and that the rest of the team would cover for the one whose child was sick. 'Just remember,' he told them, 'that next week, you might be expected to cover for the person who made it possible for you to have time off when you most needed it.' Can you imagine the team spirit and sense of camaraderie that developed between those women? They became fiercely loyal to one another and to Clive. They all knew there wasn't another boss, anywhere, who would treat them like that. They would do anything for each other and for him. Didn't anyone take advantage and stay at home when there was no need? Hardly ever. As Clive so eloquently put it: 'I never had to bring anyone back into line. The whole team is so appreciative of their working relationship with each other and with me that, if anyone does try to sucker me, all the other women simply gang up on the culprit. They either bring her back in to line themselves, or she leaves of her own accord long before it becomes a disciplinary issue.' Furthermore, the average cost of replacing a staff member who leaves (including advertising the job, interview time and training) is close to £5,000. When staff turnover is low to nonexistent, the saving to the company over the course of a year can run to a very large sum indeed, even if the company employs no more than a dozen people.

Victory is greater than mere winning

A hero is greater by far than a mere winner

Honour is everything

CHAPTER FOUR

Encouragers are Heretics

No one will disagree with me when I say creative thinking should be encouraged in every organization. Where's the heresy in that? There is none. So what's the purpose behind a chapter on a subject that's not heretical at all? Isn't this book supposed to be heretical, if not downright subversive? Let me illustrate the reason.

I was sitting in the audience at a national conference and the sales manager was encouraging the troops to believe that everyone's opinion was valued and none of us should be afraid of challenging the status quo. So far, so good. Then he said the following: 'Of course, I reserve the right to tell you you're talking bollocks!' Incredibly, that line got a laugh from the audience. Someone encourages you to express your opinion freely, but tells you that you might be told you're talking bollocks. Feel free to express your opinion, but I reserve the right not even to respect you if you express an opinion I don't agree with! Isn't that what you're really being told? He's not going to tell you you're talking bollocks as long as you're in agreement with him, is he? So how free are you to express anything? You may feel differently about this, but I felt that, either I'd better be very careful not to challenge anything, or I must be willing to accept the consequences of airing any opinion that the sales manager might think was bollocks. I chose the latter, found myself under serious pressure to leave, set up my own business, (which I'd always been too cowardly to do), and I'm now having the time of my life!

Ask anyone about leadership and they will tell you that encouraging your team is an essential element in good leadership; and so it is. The problem with encouraging freedom of expression is that, implied in that freedom, there's a willingness, on the leader's part, to listen to comments he prefers not to hear, but very much needs to be told. This takes humility. Unless we are willing to listen to opinions like this, we will simply end up surrounded by yes-men or yes-women. People willing to question the way things are done will leave and go somewhere where initiative is welcomed. When people share with me their experiences of the work place, I never cease to be amazed at how many of them say things like this:

'No one ever listens to my ideas.'

'I'm fed up of being told how to do my job by people who have lost touch with what happens at the coal face.'

'I'm tired of putting forward ideas, only to find that I never get any credit for them. Worse still, our managers claim any good ideas started with them.'

'Yes, if you really want to hack off your work force, steal all their best ideas and claim them as your own.

There are two simple tests of how committed you really are to rewarding initiative.

1. How do you respond when a member of your team challenges you with an idea you never considered before, or an idea you don't agree with?

2. How do you respond when a member of your team tries out an idea and it doesn't work? What if it not only doesn't work, but the outcome is damaging?

If the answer is that your reaction is judgmental, critical or threatening, then you are not committed to open mindedness, creative thinking, or any kind of initiative as much as you think you are. The use of initiative implies trying out ideas that have not been used before; ideas which, by definition, are untried and which carry a risk of failure. You have a responsibility to make sure that this doesn't happen, don't you? You have a responsibility to make sure it *never* happens. Or do you? Okay, this sounds like a justifiable fear, so this might be a good time to look at reasons why managers are afraid of encouraging initiative as much as they'd like to. Let's get these out in the open; then we'll look at how we can encourage and reward initiative without jeopardizing the future of the whole operation. Think about the following for a moment:

▼ If you allow untried ideas to flourish, you will be blamed for the ones that don't work.

▼ If you encourage untried ideas to flourish, the ideas will become more and more wacky, more and more irresponsible.

▼ If a junior member of staff comes up with a really great idea that even the senior management hadn't thought of, it reflects badly on them for not having thought of it themselves.

▼ The most creative staff members become a threat to the future security of their superiors.

These are really only *perceived* risks. If initiative is not encouraged, there's an even greater risk that the organization will fall behind competitors where initiative is both encouraged and rewarded. There is also the risk that, if initiative is not encouraged and rewarded within the organization, the only new ideas that will permeate are ideas that have been copied from outside organizations. While there's no harm in learning from your competition, an idea that works well for them may not work for you at all.

Some years ago, when I worked as a sales rep in the pharmaceutical industry, the company I worked for had just launched a new product. We were given our sales targets and the marketing plan. The problem I had was that, as far as I could see, the one did not follow from the other. When I asked for an explanation, I was gobsmacked at the answer I received: 'That's what Glaxo are doing.' Indeed it was, but Glaxo's products were for totally different medical conditions than the product we were launching. Glaxo's customer base bore no relation to our customer base. Glaxo's products were well established; ours was just being launched and was at a totally different stage in the sales cycle. I can't remember the exact reply I received to my question, but I seem to remember the word bollocks being in there somewhere. Never adopt any idea just because someone else is doing it. Even if everyone else is doing it does not, of itself, mean it's a good idea. Your competition might be fitting square wheels to their company cars, but that doesn't mean it would be a good idea for you to do the same. There are a lot of ideas that amount to the equivalent of fitting square wheels to company cars. As one of its slogans, The Sandler Sales Institute says the following: 'Observe what your competition is doing and do the opposite.' Why, because, when you analyse the behaviour of most organizations, what they're doing is usually not working. In the opening chapter, I gave you two very good examples, which you know to be true, of what I call 'square wheel' behaviour, which has become adopted almost universally!

Let's finish this section by examining the ways in which innovative thinking can be encouraged without risking disaster. When I was in management, I had to take the following into account when encouraging innovative thinking. (A former friend of mine has the following slogan on his business card: 'Forget the box. Just think.')

▼ Some of my staff were almost as experienced as I was. Some were very inexperienced.

▼ Some of my staff had specialist experience, which I lacked.

▼ Some of my staff were very good at coming up with ideas, but not very good when it came to evaluating them. (the *right-brain* thinkers.)

▼ Some (the *left-brain* thinkers), came up with far fewer ideas, but had thought them through very thoroughly before sharing them with me.

▼ Some ideas carried potentially disastrous consequences if they didn't work. Other ideas carried huge potential if they worked; even if they didn't, the harm done would be minimal.

▼ I made it a policy of playing devil's advocate to any idea suggested by my team, whether or not it seemed like a good idea to me. I made my team members justify their ideas; I made them think it through. They soon came to realize that all ideas would be given serious consideration. They also knew that all ideas would face serious scrutiny before receiving the green light. I had managers above me (George was one of them) whose experience and judgment I trusted implicitly. If I was unsure whether to back an idea suggested by one of my team, I could always take it to a higher authority.

While I encouraged all members of my team to come up with new ideas, I also encouraged them to share anything new with me first, for their own protection. This meant that, if the idea didn't work, the idea had been shared. It is critical to role model the following leadership approach.

▼ If the idea works, give the credit to the person who came up with the idea and do so publicly.

▼ If it doesn't work, take the responsibility yourself.

▼ Every idea will carry potential benefit and potential risk. Do not allow anyone, including yourself, to take the decision alone, especially if he/she does not have the experience or judgment to evaluate the balance between risk and benefit. A shared decision is shared responsibility. You owe it to your team not to allow them to expose themselves to acting recklessly. You owe it to your superiors to involve them if you yourself are unsure what to do.

This mutually supportive approach will only work if it is role modelled from the very top down to the most recent recruit to the team.

CHAPTER FIVE

Integrity requires Heresy

Not once, in the whole of my life, have I ever met anyone who said that honesty is unimportant to them; not once. Everyone will tell you that, in his or her organization, integrity is paramount. And yet I meet people who break their word on a daily basis and see nothing wrong with it. I run into people who do something that is totally dishonest, even illegal, and they excuse it with lame comments like these:

'Everyone else does it' or 'It's company policy' or 'My boss said I had to.'

Only one person is responsible for keeping **your** word. **You.** Only one person can be held responsible for **your** personal integrity; **that person is you.**

Be a person of your word

Don't forget that this is every bit as important when it comes to little things like the message on your mobile that *promises* that you will respond *as soon as possible.* Treat a promise the same way you treat goal setting. A promise is not really a promise unless it's a SMART promise – Specific, Measurable, Attainable, Realistic and Timely.

It's true that when you say 'as soon as possible' it hasn't exactly committed you to a specific time, but that's just the point. If it hasn't committed to you anything, it's not really a promise at all, is it? Be specific. If you're going to be busy all day, leave a message that tells your callers this. The promise might be that you will get back to them tomorrow morning. If you're going to be away for a week, tell them that you won't be answering their query until you get back and tell them when that will be. Most people won't mind the fact that you can't get back to them immediately, as long as they know why, and when they *can* expect you to get back to them. Never break a promise and never promise anything you may not be able to deliver.

Manage people's expectations. Then exceed them

One of the reasons for making SMART promises is that the other person always knows what to expect and when he can expect it. Now, here's an important tip. I was once asked by student, "How do you cope when you have so much to do that you can't handle it?" This is an excellent question; but the fact that it needed to be asked is a reflection of how many people work under the constant pressure of too much to do in too short a time.

One of the ways I manage my time so that I am hardly under pressure to deliver in an unrealistic time frame is as follows: let's say a customer asks me to prepare a write up of a course I've just completed; and let's say that I reckon I can complete the task within three days. I *do not* promise that I will get it to him in three days. Instead, I will say something like this: 'I'm really very busy for the next few days. Is it going to be a problem to you if I can't get the document to you in less than a week?" Now, here's the point. It is very rare indeed for this to be a problem. A week is usually perfectly acceptable, so I'm under no pressure. In fact, when I do get the report to him in three days, he's over the moon. Not only did I keep my promise, but I exceeded his expectations. In the event that he *must* have the document the next day, I'm going to bust a gut to meet his requirement; but this hardly ever happens. The other advantage of giving myself more time than I really need, as a matter of policy, is this: it sometimes happens that something comes my way completely out of the blue, something which requires my urgent attention and which I could not possibly have foreseen. Because I always allow myself more time for a task than I expect I will need, I can deal with the unexpected without breaking my word, or having to apologize for not doing what I promised. He was expecting me to take a week anyway. He's still delighted. Most people take twice as long as they promised.

Keep within the law. Do what is right, even if it's not illegal.

A young couple recently bought their first house (another true story, by the way). This meant moving out of the flat they were renting before the contracts were exchanged. It also meant buying furniture for the new house before they were in a position to move in. While buying a bed from a well-known retail store, they explained this and were told that this would not be a problem. 'Just let us know when you're ready to move in. We'll hold onto it until then,' they were told. Money changed hands and when contracts were exchanged, they contacted the store and asked them to deliver the bed they had paid for five weeks previously. 'I'm terribly sorry,' the shop assistant said. "You took so long we sold it to someone else.' Needless to say, the couple were far from pleased with this, especially as they'd explained, before paying, that there was going to be a delay. 'I'm terribly sorry,' came the indignant reply, 'but we're not a storage facility you know!' Excuse me! This is flat out wrong on several counts:

▼ Once you've paid for something, it's your property. The fact that it may not yet be in your possession, does not alter that fact. If it's your property, selling it to someone else is against the law.

▼ You may not be a storage facility; but you said you were happy to hold onto the bed until contracts were exchanged. That was the agreement. If it wasn't acceptable, you should have made that clear at the time. Even if it were not illegal, you still broke your word. You have still behaved dishonourably.

▼ Note the tone of the reply. Saying 'We're not a storage facility' tries to imply that the customer is the one who's at fault! Not only was this action totally out of order, but the store saw nothing wrong with what they'd done; even suggesting that the couple were to blame.

It's a funny old world we're living in today. This sort of thing is going on all the time and I'll bet you have similar stories of your own. I've talked a lot about conflict avoidance and I stand by what I say that looking for fights is a terrible waste of energy. Besides, you almost always end up making yourself far more miserable than anyone else. But when it comes to your personal integrity, you must not compromise. Your personal integrity has to be non-negotiable and everyone around you needs to know that it's non-negotiable. This includes your customers, the people who report to you and even your own boss. No one ought to be in any doubt that this is an area where you absolutely refuse to be pushed around.

Here are a couple of examples of situations which can become extremely compromising if you allow them to. Two will be enough for you to get the idea.

A van driver is asked to deliver goods to several customers, but the time available does not allow him to do this without breaking speed limits. Breaking speed limits is illegal. You cannot be required by your employer to break the law. If you get caught on a speed camera, you will get no sympathy from a magistrate simply by saying 'My boss said I had to." Encouraging someone else to break the law is itself an offence.

Your work colleagues are fiddling their expenses and there's peer-group pressure on you to do the same. 'Everyone else is,' they say.

'So? What's that got to do with anything?' you ask.

'No one will ever know.'

Yes they will. You will.

'Don't be a wimp!' they say.

But standing up for what is right does not make you a wimp. It takes guts to stand up for what you know is right, especially when everyone else is doing the opposite. You're probably the bravest person in the building.

Leaders always stand up for what is right;
and you're an aspiring leader, right?

CHAPTER SIX

Personality Profiling, NLP and other Heresies

My friend Gerwyn and I were at the bar. I was buying Gerwyn a drink to celebrate him being sales champion in his division. Gerwyn was one of the most experienced and respected members of the sales team, a guy that many of the younger members of the field force would turn to for guidance. We both had cause to celebrate because my territory had just hit £1m, the first in my division to do so. Gerwyn was pretty streetwise and as we sipped beer together he said to me with that lovely Welsh valleys lilt of his:

'You and I are an embarrassment to them really.'

'How d'you mean?' I asked.

'Well,' he answered, 'let's be honest, Barry. If you and I were applying for a job with the company now, we wouldn't even get an interview. They'd perform a personality profile on us, and since neither of us is a Driver or an Expressive, we wouldn't fit the bill, would we now?'

I laughed, because he was right. A lot of managers these days decide in advance which personalities are ideal for a particular position; anyone who doesn't fit goes no further. Once you progress towards leadership, you're going to hear a lot about personality profiling, neurolinguistic programming (NLP) and transactional analysis;

and it's all good stuff. It's very good stuff. As a qualified personality profiler, no one believes in the value of profiling more than I do. I also believe that, like any tool, it should be used with common sense and for the right purpose. Along with psychometric testing and NLP, it's becoming one of latest business fads. And, like anything that becomes a fad, the use to which it is put is sometimes inappropriate.

Three areas where personality profiling can be very misleading

Shortly, I will summarize what I consider to be the invaluable purposes to which personality profiling can be applied. First, however, I want to cover three areas in which personality profiling can be very misleading and where even the professionals may be seeking to mislead you.

The first of these is deciding whether a personality equips a candidate for a specific job. This is not to say that certain personalities are unsuited to certain jobs; they are. A highly extrovert, impulsive character will make a disastrous air traffic controller! But do you think that a person of this temperament is ever likely to apply for such a post in the first place? In the very unlikely event that such a candidate did answer a job advert for such a post, do you really think that an experienced manager would be unable to spot such a glaring mismatch? Do you really require the services of someone like me to point out something so obvious? I wouldn't insult you by taking your money, even if you were willing to pay me! The point is that most people know instinctively if they are totally unsuitable for a job and they will not go for it in the first place. If a candidate is unsuitable, this is usually because they lack sufficient experience, qualifications or motivation; but this may be true *whatever personality you are dealing with.*

I recently fell into conversation with a middle manager who had just completed a round of first interviews on a bunch of candidates. With some irritation in his voice, he told me that some of the candidates, with whom he was particularly impressed, and whom he would have been delighted to work with, had not been offered a second interview, in spite of his recommendation that they should be. And the grounds on which they were eliminated? Their personalities didn't fit the job description. 'It seems to me,' he said, 'that we've become obsessed with this sort of thing. I'm not convinced that we don't end up weeding out some of the best people and for all the wrong reasons.'

The truth is that most jobs do not require a particular personality type. The decision to deselect certain candidates, primarily on the basis of a personality profile, carries the risk that you end up with a very unbalanced team. Would you think it a good idea to adopt a selection process that eliminated people who brought the following clusters of qualities to your team?

▼ A sense of adventure, combined with determination, creativity and innovation?

▼ Great imagination, combined with spontaneity, inspiration and a sense of fun?

▼ Stability, harmony, calmness and security?

▼ An analytical mind, objectivity, consistency and logic?

On the other hand, would you want an entire team comprising only one of these four examples?

When personality profiling becomes an end in itself, there is a real danger that, along with psychometric testing and neurolinguistic programming it will become discredited.

The second danger in selection by profiling is not so obvious. Whatever your personality, you can project that personality in a mature or an immature way and every one of us occasionally goes off the scale. When we do, it's ugly and I'm sure you know what I mean.

Some professionals will not only list what the mature version looks like, but what the same personality looks like in its immature form, regardless of whether the candidate displays this tendency or not. I've seen this happen; and the interviewer can end up bewildered and wondering if any candidate is safe to employ! Let me tell you this. When a person is acting immature, you can tell. There are clues; you don't need a professional to point out something so obvious. The value of profiling is that it informs you what strengths a person with that personality will bring to the team, how they will strengthen the team in times of crisis and how you, as a leader, should treat them in order to get the very best out of them (see below).

The third pitfall follows from the dangerous assumption that people of similar temperament will make the best business partners. A vicar needed to raise funds for church maintenance. His congregation included three very successful businessmen. These three, all men of action and real go-getters, had very similar outlooks on life and were great friends outside work. The obvious thing to do, the vicar thought, was to put them together on the case. It proved to be a disaster. All three wanted to take control and be in charge. After all, that's how they ran their respective businesses. The project quickly fell apart. It does not follow that people who get on well socially will work harmoniously as a team. Any professional will tell you that some of the worst personality clashes occur between people of similar temperament.

Believe it or not, this can be just as much a problem with the reserved, people-oriented types whose instinct is to avoid conflict at all costs. I once represented our church at an away day. During the afternoon session, we broke into small discussion groups and I was nominated to lead one of these and report our conclusions to the group as a whole. Little did I realize that I had a whole team of S-types, none of whom wanted to share an opinion in case it conflicted with someone else's idea. Although I am an S-type myself, they almost drove me mad – I felt like killing them. In fact, it was a very valuable lesson because it taught me how irritatingly indecisive S-types can appear and that perhaps I come across like that sometimes, especially to the more dynamic D-types. (If you don't know what an S-type or a D-type is, don't worry about it. But maybe it would be a good idea to find out.)

The insights a personality profiler can give about your team

Here then is a selection of insights a professional personality profiler will be able to give about you and your team:

▼ The qualities that make you special.

▼ The qualities that make each member of your team special.

▼ Your blind spots; the behaviours in others that may trigger an overreaction on your part.

▼ The blind spots of people in your team.

▼ The behaviours on your part, and on the part of other team members, that may trigger inappropriate responses from colleagues.

▼ That there is no such thing as a bad personality.

▼ How to value the role and contribution of each member of your team.

▼ How to inspire, listen to and respect contrasting styles.
  How to be an exceptional leader.

▼ How understanding contrasting personalities will keep you in touch with what moves people. If you're not in touch with what moves them, they simply won't move – just in case you haven't noticed!

▼ A framework for working with other people so their egos and yours remain intact.

▼ An understanding of what each member of your team would like to impress you with. Tailor your praise accordingly.

▼ How to become highly skilled at making each member of your team feel that he/she amounts to something.

▼ How to kill a relationship stone dead… and how to avoid doing so.

That's rather a long list isn't it? Are any of these issues unimportant to you?

It is within your power to make others feel **important, liked, appreciated and respected.** Do this and they will regard you as the cleverest, most personable individual they've ever met.

It is a power that never runs out.
So be generous with it.

CHAPTER SEVEN

Teamwork:
One Big Heresy

It's time for the company conference, a time to review sales trends, who's on target for a bonus and who's going to miss their targets. There's also time for team building. A coach takes a group of sales reps down to the seafront where they disgorge onto the sand for a game of beach volleyball. Totally excluded, the longest standing and most loyal sales rep, who is four years short of retirement and still recovering from a hip replacement, is left sitting on the sidelines catching a death of cold. We call this TEAM BUILDING.

A chief executive concludes his presentation with a rousing motivational speech to his troops: 'We can be proud that we're the fastest growing company in our market. We can be proud that we have more new products in our pipeline than any of our competitors. We can be proud that our future is secure.' They have smashed their sales targets and every objective measure of performance would seem to indicate that, if you want to join this industry, this is the company to be with. You would think so wouldn't you? But only one employee in six will still be working for him in 12 months' time. WHY?

A grim-faced sales manager addresses his sales team. This is not the annual conference. This meeting has been called because the company is experiencing severe production difficulties for which there might be no immediate solution. It's going to be extremely difficult to meet customer demand. There will be no Christmas bonuses this year. In fact, there will be no bonuses of any kind. He is not even in a position to guarantee everyone's jobs. He ends his address by telling his troops that, if any of them feels that, in the interests of their family security, they must seek alternative employment, he will not stand in their way. At a time when the company is close to going under, not one member of his team seeks alternative employment. WHY?

What made the difference? Here's a clue. It had nothing to do with abseiling down cliff faces or building rafts out of oil drums and sticky tape!

Slaughtering the sacred cows of teambuilding

Everyone knows what I'm talking about. We meet this lip service attitude everywhere and not just towards team building. *There is a prevailing belief that there is a short cut to almost any kind of success.* Experience teaches us otherwise. Let's take a look at a few illusions, the sacred cows of team building. Here are a few prime examples:

▼ If people are talking to each other, they're a team

▼ If people are friends, they're a team

▼ As long as people are not in conflict, they're a team

▼ If people are being nice to each other, they're a team

Really? That's all there is to it? Hardly!

That's like saying that because people live in the same road, you have a community. Communities have shared values. They value each other as people, not just for what they produce. The same is true of great teams. The value they place on their relationship with one another goes way beyond mere productivity. While respect can be offered without knowing much about one another, trust and loyalty are earned. That takes time and it's not going to be earned riding around muddy fields on quad bikes.

'Superficiality is the curse of our age,' says Richard Foster. 'Depth comes slowly;' or, as John Ortberg puts it, 'You can't have maturity microwaved.'

Organizing activities where the purpose is to have fun is a very good idea. Activities which encourage bonding between people who are already totally committed to one another are a thoroughly good idea; but let's not confuse them with what's required to build people into a team in the first place!

LEVEL ONE: *The dysfunctional level*

At this level, the members of the group don't even know each other, and don't even know whether they're going to like one another or not! They will achieve next to nothing unless they progress to the next level.

LEVEL TWO: *The co-operative level*

At this level, they are getting on okay. There are no obvious tensions and they will work together to complete a task. On the other hand, they can hardly be described as friends and probably wouldn't choose one another as colleagues. This is still a group rather than a team and it wouldn't take much to divide them.

LEVEL THREE: *The friendship level*

At this level, everyone likes everyone else. Working together is fun; they probably meet up socially after work too. Their friendship would probably continue even if the company no longer existed.

LEVEL FOUR: *The self-sacrificial level*

At this level, there is total commitment to each other's well-being and the organization's well-being. This extends to the point where each team member will put the best interests of other team members ahead of his or her own best interests. They are more than a team: they are a band of brothers and sisters whose shared values are something they defend and fight for – tooth and nail if called on to do so. In the **ultimate example,** they will risk their lives for one another and say it was worth it!

Only when a community faces adversity do we discover what it's really made of. Only when its members face adversity shoulder to shoulder can you be sure that a team has reached the fourth level. Adversity, not success, reveals an individual's real values; and the team's real values. Do your team members blame or support each other when their backs are against the wall? Do tough times divide them or unite them? In a crisis, does argument break out or do they stand shoulder to shoulder? Which behaviour are **you** role modelling? You're supposed to be the leader aren't you?

If you think this is just an exercise in idealism, let me ask you a question or two. Have you ever watched one of those extraordinary tennis matches where a player is two sets down, facing three match points against him and goes on to win? Let's talk about this situation for a moment and consider in particular why the crowd loves to see a comeback like this:

- ▼ Even the crowd has accepted that the situation is hopeless.

- ▼ It takes enormous courage and resolve to come back from a situation that everyone regards as hopeless.

- ▼ Winning from a position like this is going to be a long haul.

That's what makes it heroic. And crowds love heroes. **Crowds are inspired by heroics and so are teams.**

Let's now consider a slightly different situation. The team is a mixed doubles partnership. They're also facing three match points against them. The reason they're in this situation is that the guy has been playing well below his best. Now here's the question: how should his partner respond? We all know the answer. If the partnership is to have any chance at all of a comeback, she must encourage him. He doesn't need to be told he's underperforming; he knows it. Her role must be to encourage him, to believe in him in spite of his underperformance and to stop his underperformance affecting his morale. What will happen if she doesn't? They may as well forfeit the match without a fight. Am I right? Let's suppose, though, that they survive the three match points, go on to win the second set and are back in the match. They have a break point that will put them ahead in the deciding set and serving for the match when the girl, faced with an open court, hammers the ball into the base of the net. How should her partner respond? Should he yell at her, telling her how useless she is and how he can't imagine how he puts up with her? Have you ever seen a player treat a partner like that? Look, she knows it was a wretched shot. She's already angry with herself. His role must be to help her get over it and concentrate on the next point. The issue is this: both partners need to know that the other's support is unconditional. They don't think they can count on each other no matter what, they know it.

Have you ever seen a partnership succeed at anything unless this was the case? So why is this kind of support so rare in business? Well, you may say, in business we don't have the luxury of this approach. There's the bottom line to think about. Listen, do you mean to tell me there's no money in professional sport? Are you really trying to tell me there's no room for this kind of behaviour unless there's nothing at stake? Oh come on! The strongest bonds of all are formed between people whose lives depend on the support they get from one another. So, here's the final issue. Does your system of appraisal encourage your players to come back from a hopeless situation or does it encourage writing them off as underperformers at the first sign of not hitting their targets? If it's the latter, how are you going to recognize the real heroes in your organization? How are you going to encourage responsible risk taking? How are you going to develop the next generation of leaders? Here's how:

1. Forget about building a team; build a fellowship – a community.

2. Teams have goals. A fellowship has a cause.

3. A goal may unite your people, but they will sacrifice themselves for a cause.

4. A goal may consume you. A cause will nurture you, inspire you and set you on fire.

Let me end this heresy with a few favourite quotations:

> *'When you are looking for a team to reach any summit, put forth a picture of the mountain, your mountain, and let climbers break down your door to join the ascent. Look for tenacity and fortitude to stay, but* <u>*look, most of all, for those who cannot imagine leaving.*</u>*"* (my underline)

Todd Skinner

> *'If you are afraid that the team is not equal to the mountain, let the mountain make them equal to it.'*

Todd Skinner

'If a team looks ordinary on paper, that is no reason to choose a smaller mountain. The mountain can make them extraordinary. The team should sign on, not to see if the mountain can be climbed, but to climb it. If the summit is worthy of their best efforts, it will carry them beyond who they thought they were, toward who they are meant to become.'

Todd Skinner

But always, in the best interests of everyone, remember that some people will never catch the vision and you must not hold the entire team back in the hope that they will, if you give them long enough. Inviting people to share your vision does not mean you have to leave your brains behind! Common sense and other members of the team will tell you when enough is long enough. (See also Chapter 11.)

Now let's get on with the next heresy.

CHAPTER EIGHT

Conflict results from Heresy

It takes no skill whatsoever to get into a fight. Anyone can do it. The question is: why on earth would you want to? The consequences of getting into quarrels at work are bad. Here are just a few:

- ▼ You lose the respect of your staff.

- ▼ You reduce your chances of hitting your bottom line.

- ▼ You risk costly litigation.

- ▼ You fail to build your people into a team.

- ▼ You run the risk of low staff morale.

- ▼ You risk high staff turnover and the huge costs involved in replacing them (£5,000 at the time of writing, to replace one member of staff).

- ▼ You get a reputation for being a dictator.

How are these in your best interests? They're not, are they?

There are companies whose whole business is resolving conflict. The problem with conflict resolution, as opposed to conflict avoidance, is that conflict resolution may well involve a tribunal, expensive litigation or simply a settlement out of court. Even if all these are avoided, the damage, in terms of loss of trust, has already been done. Frequently, the best way out is a parting of the ways. The damage this does to relationships in the work place, in the home or anywhere else is incalculable in both human and financial terms. **Avoiding it altogether must surely be the goal for every one of us.**

The key to avoiding conflict

The following rule should be agreed by every single member of your team, whatever his/her rank or position:

"It is forbidden to say anything unkind or do anything hurtful to any other member of the team."

It's a rule that should never be broken. However, the person who is capable of keeping this rule unfailingly has not been born; which leads us to a rather bewildering paradox:

- ▼ Is the rule pointless because it's bound to be broken?
- ▼ If so, should hurtful behaviour be allowed or ignored?

The answer is no on both counts. What we need to do is two things:

1. Minimize the likelihood of hurtful behaviour occurring.
2. Introduce a second rule to ensure that permanent damage to relationships is avoided when the rule is broken.

If we are going to ensure that hurtful behaviour is exceptional, we need to be aware of the most frequent reasons it happens in the first place.

Bring to mind for a moment a recent conflict situation in your life, whether you were personally involved or not. The chances are high that no one wanted conflict – they rarely do. So why, and how, does conflict happen so often? The answer is that, in almost all cases, **someone's ego was bruised, someone's identity was threatened, or someone's values were compromised.**

Disagreement is not the same as conflict; disagreement can be healthy. Someone once said that the day you and I have the same opinion on every subject, one of us is unnecessary!

The concept of *being out of integrity*

At this point I want to introduce a concept that you may not have come across before: *the concept of being out of integrity.* Let's start with a couple of very simple examples. Suppose someone comes up to you and says 'Hi Mary' (but your name is not Mary) or 'Hi Colin' (when your name is not Colin). You may be amused, but more likely you'll be slightly irritated or even quite annoyed at someone getting your name wrong. *That's not who you are. You are out of integrity.* This sort of misunderstanding is usually put right quite easily and, usually, no real damage has been done to the relationship.

Now let's look at another example that's easy to understand but far more damaging. You're with a group of other managers. They are not your close friends, but you want their respect; it might be beneficial to your career prospects. All's well until they try to involve you in fiddling your expenses, exploiting your staff or something else you know to be wrong. Suddenly, you experience an internal conflict. Whatever course of action you chose, you're either going to lose their support or you're going to compromise your personal values. By putting you in this situation, you feel you can't win. The whole situation is threatening and you probably feel resentment at being put in this situation. You feel difficulty trusting these people from now on and, while you may not actually fall out with them, you will probably try to distance yourself from them in future. You were placed in a situation where you were invited *not to be true to yourself. You were out of integrity.*

In the last example there were clear right and wrong options. However, many conflict situations arise where no one is clearly in the right. This is where an understanding of the way different personalities prioritize things helps enormously. For example, Dave, a sales rep, is a dynamic, go-getter who has generated a potential order for his company. But the contract needs to be drawn up in watertight legal language. His customer, Gavin, also a dynamic go-getter, wants to proceed within five working days. Claire, whose responsibility it is to draw up the contract, is a meticulous personality and insists that the contract cannot be rushed in case the wording leaves loopholes. She tells Dave that she cannot complete the paperwork in less than a week. Dave complains that this might mean the contract being lost to a competitor; a delay might cost him a bonus of £2,000. Who is in the right? There's no obvious correct answer, but *both may feel out of integrity with themselves if they compromise.* The chances are that both Dave and Claire think the other is being extremely unreasonable and simply insisting on getting their own way.

Let's look at another example. Denise is a company director. The company has been through difficult times and Denise, being very much a task-oriented person, has decided that right now the most important task is to get the company back on an even keel. The time has come to announce staff redundancies. Sarah, her HR manager, is a people person through and through; for Sarah, such a course of action is unthinkable and heartless. Denise and Sarah have always had the greatest respect for each other, but now there is a serious problem. Staff have been loyal to the company and to take away their livelihoods is a betrayal. Sarah wants no part in such an insensitive decision. Denise points out that without redundancies the firm may well go into liquidation, in which case *everyone* will be out of a job, not just a handful. Is Denise right? Is Sarah right? You tell me. One thing is for certain: *both feel out of integrity with the other's approach.* Aggression on Denise's part won't resolve the matter; neither will Sarah's stubborn resistance. Denise needs to recognize that in her own approach there is a serious threat to Sarah's personal integrity. Sarah must recognize that the same is true of her solution as far as Denise is concerned. **If they fail to do this, their future relationship may never be the same.**

This is a classic example of two contrasting personalities discovering that there are aspects of their own personalities that each regards as a key strength, but which, under certain circumstances, can be perceived as a fatal weakness by the other. If you're going to avoid unnecessary conflict, it's terribly important to understand that some of the things you like most about yourself may, in certain situations, be extremely irritating to a person with a contrasting personality.

Causes of conflict

Conflict can arise for many different reasons, but without exception all the following result in someone's ego being bruised, someone's identity coming under threat and a feeling that compromise is not possible without coming out of integrity with oneself.

- ▼ Conflicting values.
- ▼ Conflicting priorities.
- ▼ Concluding that your needs and the other person's needs are mutually exclusive.
- ▼ Confusing willingness to compromise your position with compromising your personal integrity.
- ▼ Forming a false perception of another person's intentions and motives.
- ▼ Not listening to the concerns of others or the emotion behind them.
- ▼ Forming a low opinion of people who don't share your views.
- ▼ Attributing unworthy motives to those who don't share our views.
- ▼ Allowing fear, anger or even hatred to become our controlling emotions.

▼ Unreasonable expectations.

▼ Failure to live up to a *reasonable* expectation.
   (What is reasonable?)

Conflict can result from clashing differences or competing similarities.

It's a long list and makes the subject sound very complicated. Let's simplify things a bit shall we? Conflict occurs when a person is hurting, feeling threatened or feels offended. Conflict will be avoided as long as we don't hurt someone else's ego, don't threaten their identity and don't offend their sense of justice and fair play.

Notice, however, that conflict avoidance will be achieved whatever the cause as long as the following rule is always observed:

> *"It is forbidden to say anything unkind or do anything hurtful to any other member of the team."*

CONFLICT RESOLUTION (reproduced by kind permission of Spirit of Peace)

'Peace from the barrel of a gun' is a phrase which has stuck in my mind since the war in Iraq. The temptation to use violent means to blast opponents into submission or to exterminate them is one that is all too frequently resorted to on an international level, with horrifying human and environmental consequences.

Temporary 'peace' may ensue as the opposition is weakened or obliterated but this rarely leads to a true and lasting peace, as the participants become victim and oppressor and a new cycle of revenge or fighting for freedom begins. Even when a form of peace is achieved the cost is enormous and the resultant 'peace' is fragile and unstable.

So what of our own lives and communities? Are we tempted in subtle ways to impose 'peace' in turbulent situations? Stereotypical images come to mind here: the mother beleaguered by squabbling offspring, the nagging wife or demanding husband, the overbearing boss or passive - aggressive employee.

Often there is a temptation to find quick but temporary fixes by some sort of subtle pressure or force, which might involve exclusion, avoidance, some form of physical or verbal abuse or threatening silence, rather than find a way to build a bridge of understanding.

The first step to building a bridge of understanding is often a backward step, one which takes us out of range of the source of aggravation and allows us to reflect and see a wider picture and the root causes rather than remain locked into dispute or avoidance.

As always, when people who are seen as representing different sides in a conflict share a platform, there are tough issues to be faced and much stimulus for reflection and action is engendered.

After a step backwards, creating a safe space to hear the story of 'the other' might be a step towards resolution of conflict.

The Sufis advise us to speak only after our words have managed to pass through three gates: At the first gate, we ask ourselves, 'Are these words true?' At the second gate, we ask, 'Are they necessary?' At the last gate, we ask, 'Are they kind?'"

Give your people permission to challenge you

Lasting peace cannot be built on falsehood, in the workplace any more than anywhere else. One of the most effective ways of avoiding conflict, at home or work, is to give your team (it could be your family, including your children) permission to challenge you if they ever feel that you are getting things wrong. I will never forget the day one of my teenage sons said to me, 'Dad, you're so focused on business success that you're neglecting Mum.' It must have taken guts for him to say that to me; but he was right. What if I'd never realized? What if he'd never pointed out to me what I was doing? It scares me to think what might have happened to my marriage if he hadn't acted on the permission he knew he had to challenge me in this way.

Giving permission of this kind has a number of benefits:

▼ People feel respected.

▼ They feel that you genuinely care about them and their feelings.

▼ They feel that you are truly committed to doing what is right and in the best interests of the whole team, even if it means accepting that you are not behaving as you should. It takes humility to accept that, sometimes, the problem is you. But sometimes it is!

▼ They are no longer afraid to tell you what you need to hear, even though you may not want to hear it.

▼ They feel confident that they will be listened to.

▼ When they do challenge you, they will not feel a need to become all stroppy and bolshie! They will challenge you in the respectful way that you deserve.

NOTE: The challenge will not always be justified and you don't have to agree every time.

Conflict is threatening. People react to threats in one of two ways:

▼ They fight back.

▼ They try to escape the threat.

Unfortunately, and no matter how skilfully you deal with other people, conflict is bound to happen occasionally. Whenever this happens, you must learn from it. You do so by addressing two questions:

1. What rule was violated here?
2. How can I handle a similar situation better next time?

Handling people who really are difficult

Okay, but what do you do when people shout at you? What do you do when they use sarcasm? What do you do when they use threats?

How to handle people who shout at you

Why do people shout? Usually, people shout because they're angry. The question is, what works with an angry person? Maybe we should start with what *never* works. Never tell them to calm down. Never infer that you think they're being unreasonable (even if they are). Have you ever been told to calm down when you were absolutely furious about something? How did you feel? You felt even angrier didn't you? If you aren't feeling aggressive before, you feel almost homicidal when someone tells you to calm down and not to overreact! Anger is one of the most powerful emotions; you're playing with fire if you tell people to control themselves. The secret is to find a way to change the emotion of the other person. This relies on understanding why they're angry in the first place. Let's look at the main reasons people may be angry and deal with each in turn.

They have good reason to be angry – someone let them down; someone broke a promise; someone prevented them from achieving something that was important to them. There are lots of examples. This, however, is not the only reason they're shouting. They're also shouting because they have decided that, unless they get aggressive, they will get a brush off, that they are not going get justice any other way. So the first move is to demonstrate, as clearly as you can, that you have every sympathy with the way they feel: 'Really. No wonder you're annoyed. I'd be furious if that had happened to me.' The problem still requires a solution, but now there's no further need to feel angry. They have an ally. Someone understands. Someone does not think their anger is unreasonable. Immediately, they begin to calm down. When you are being so reasonable, it's very difficult for them to maintain their aggressive posturing without seeing themselves as the unreasonable party. Now you can concentrate on the solution. It might sound like this:

'Look, I'm really very sorry for what's happened. There is no excuse for it.' You follow this with something like this:

'What do you see as the best solution from your point of view?'

or

'What would you like me to do to put things right, assuming I'm in a position to do that for you?'

If they can't suggest anything, you might say something like this:

'Suppose I were to do this for you. Would that be a fair outcome for you, given that we can't change what's happened?'

You can use this approach and accept responsibility for putting things right even if you're not personally to blame. If you are, you must admit it and apologize.

But suppose the other person's anger is not justified – what if they are being thoroughly unreasonable? Then what? Again we have to understand why the person might be acting like this. One reason might be that they know they're in the wrong but don't know how to acknowledge this without feeling put down. There's a subtly different version of the above, which can be used here. It goes like this:

'I would be angry too, if I felt that was what had been done to me.' Again, you're empathizing with the anger; but notice the difference. You're not accepting that his feeling is necessarily appropriate. You then follow this as follows:

'I'm not sure I understand why you feel the way you do. Can you help me to understand?' You're showing a willingness to listen to their explanation; yet you're challenging them, in a non-threatening way, to justify their feelings. If they begin to struggle, once their own explanation begins to make them feel uncomfortable, now is the time to rescue them. If we don't, they'll flip from being very aggressive to extremely defensive, which will also get in the way of a positive outcome.

'I see where you're coming from. As I see it, we want the fairest outcome for both of us. This is not about blaming anyone is it? Can we try to agree what is the fairest outcome, for both of us?

Even though the other person is in the wrong, they're being let off the hook. They don't deserve it, but that's what's happening and they're relieved. They're also being offered a sensible option. As long as they're prepared to be as fair to you as you are to them, you'll be happy. Only the most unreasonable person won't respond to that.

Handling people who use sarcasm

'I suppose this is the way you treat all your customers is it?'

'I see that your company policy includes downright ineptitude!'

This sort of thing is not only very irritating, it's also extremely provocative. It's meant to be. Deliberately or otherwise, the intention is to wind you up and provoke you into losing your cool so as to gain the upper hand. They *will* gain the upper hand if you allow yourself to fall for this tactic. It's a professional foul; but what are you going to do to avoid swallowing the bait?

Rule number one is to stay calm. Inside, you're seething, but stay calm. Sarcasm is a symptom of annoyance; so we can handle it in a similar way that we handled anger.

'Madam, it sounds as if you're annoyed about something. Would you mind telling me what it is?' Be prepared for a second round of sarcasm.

'You shouldn't need to ask why I'm annoyed. I would have thought it was obvious. Do they employ morons around here?' This is always said with a really unpleasant smirk that makes you want to smack her in the chops! Don't!

Instead, try something like this:

'Madam, I'm confident that you came in here wanting a solution to the problem, whatever that is. Before I can know what the solution might look like, I do need you to tell me what's gone wrong.' Stay calm but be firm. You are helping her to realize that continued sarcasm is getting in the way of the very thing she wants – a solution to whatever went wrong. Whether anger takes the form of aggression or sarcasm, your best move is to focus on what's gone wrong and how it went wrong; and what needs to be done to put things right.

Handling people who get their retaliation in first

This is simply another version of the person who shouts at you, except that this time, instead of shouting, they use a threat. It goes something like this:

'If you don't sort this out immediately, I'm going to write a complaint to your manager with a request that you lose your job.'

As with any form of aggression, this is deliberate intimidation. It's essential that he's made to realize that you're not going to fall for it and that you are not *going* to be intimidated. On the other hand, as before, you *are* prepared to look for a sensible solution.

'Sir, I'm sure you wouldn't be making a threat like that without a very good reason. Would you like to tell me what's happened?'

Note the words 'without a very good reason'. What you're doing is assuming that he is, whatever your personal feelings are towards this guy, a perfectly reasonable person. You are inviting him to live up to that. Once you've established what lies behind the threat, you can then decide that (a) his complaint is justified, or (b) that it's not.

Then you work towards a solution in much the same way as you did in the first example, the person who shouted at you.

Handling differences of opinion

Unless you belong to a team made up entirely of yes-men or yes-women, differences of opinion are not only inevitable, they're healthy. However, all too often they lead to feelings of anger, frustration and loss of respect. At this point, I'd like to tell you about a remarkable interview I heard on radio many years ago. Two people were being interviewed: one was the master of hounds from the Cotswold Hunt; the other was the leader of the Hunt Saboteurs.

When two people with such opposing viewpoints are being interviewed, you expect the sparks to really fly. You expect the language to deteriorate and become hostile bordering on abusive! This was clearly what the interviewer was expecting and hoping for. It makes good radio, right? What was remarkable was that this was not what happened at all. In spite of the fact that neither backed down on what they stood for, there was no animosity between them. One of them even went so far as to say that they sent Christmas cards to each other. Moreover, on the day of a hunt, both of them took responsibility for ensuring that their own followers avoided overreacting in a way that might lead to things getting out of hand.

When the interview was over, I analysed what had been going on and what rules the two parties had observed that allowed them to stick to their guns without things turning nasty. Whether they were doing so consciously or not, I don't know, but I have used the technique many times since and it almost always works. Here's how to approach someone whose opinion is so opposed to your own that conflict might appear to be unavoidable. You say something like this:

'I'm having difficulty with your point of view. Please can you explain the thinking behind what you believe. I may change my point of view, but I cannot promise to do so. I do promise to do my best to understand where you're coming from. I want to respect you, even if we still can't agree.' This removes the threat of conflict while leaving you free to stick to your guns if you still believe you're right. You're offering respect, not a guaranteed climb down!

The Forgiveness Rule

I'd now like to quote from the *Spirit of Peace* newsletter again:

> *'Our personal truth and perceptions are*
> *partly a product of our identity.*
> *We must approach the truth with the*
> *humility and vulnerability to recognize that*
> *our personal truth is but part of a larger*
> *truth. We need to be willing to modify*
> *our understanding, even when this is a*
> *challenge to our sense of identity.*
> *Peace making involves risk and being open*
> *to truths which challenge our identity, our*
> *beliefs and our sense of belonging.*
> *This can be extremely anxiety provoking.'*

Before concluding this section, I'd like you to take part in a short exercise. Imagine a child who has done something really naughty. The child is afraid of being found out; there's going to be serious trouble. Maybe what the child deserves is a good hiding, but that's not what happens. Instead, mum or dad just holds the child very close and speaks, not angrily, but softly. The parents are disappointed. The child feels ashamed, knowing he/she let the family down and yet the overwhelming feeling is a feeling of forgiveness and unconditional love. Now ask yourself the following four questions.

1. What effect did this have on the child?

2. What effect did it have on the child's relationship with the parents?

3. What effect did it have on any brothers and sisters?

4. Were the parents right to treat the child the way they did – or should they have walloped the living daylights out of the kid?

If you believe they were right, why doesn't the same principle apply in the workplace? At what age do you think it *does* become okay to kick the daylights out of your people – even when they deserve it?

Bad feeling can ALWAYS be overcome as long as one person is willing to say, 'I'm sorry' and the other is equally willing to say, 'It's okay, I forgive you.' There has to be agreement in the team that **this rule** will never, ever, under any circumstances be broken. If this is understood the team can recover from just about any misunderstanding or mistake. If not, trust can be undermined permanently. There **will** be such agreement if the team leaders are willing to role model this type of forgiving example. As a leader, you *have to be ready* to do just this, and there will be times when it is far from easy. **It is not going to happen unless you do,** and without it, members of a team are always going to wonder what will happen the day one of them messes up.

The real test of your loyalty is the way you treat your team when they have messed up, failed to hit a goal or there is a serious difference of opinion. Some people will argue that willingness to forgive simply encourages other people to take advantage of you. My answer to this is that *unconditional forgiveness is not the same thing as unconditional approval.* **Forgiveness is one of the highest forms of personal responsibility for the well-being of every team member, but no one with the well-being of the team at heart will encourage irresponsible behaviour. To do so is not leadership.**

CHAPTER NINE

The Heretic Presenter

Here's a question for you. How many times have you suffered death by PowerPoint? Maybe your answer will be different from mine, but here's my answer: 'Just about every time I sit through a presentation!' This applies, by the way, whether the presentation is delivered by a student or a company chief executive. In fact, the chief executive's presentation will be no better (and maybe worse) than the student's.

Now for a second question: when was the last time you sat through a presentation which did *not* involve PowerPoint? That's weird isn't it? Hardly anyone ever presents without using PowerPoint, even though we all know it's been the death of almost every presentation we've ever sat through. So why do we continue to do something that doesn't work? If ever there was an example of square wheel philosophy, this has to be it!

Do you really need PowerPoint?

Maybe we need to examine the thinking behind using PowerPoint. Then we'll take a hard look at whether this thinking holds water. The thinking behind using PowerPoint is this: when we're told something we remember... *this* much. When we're told something and we're shown a picture of it, we remember *this* much, plus a bit; and if the image moves and pretty pictures appear and disappear and animated bullet points appear from left and right of the screen there's no telling how much we're going to remember! That's the theory, right, and there are statistics to back it up.

Now let's think about a situation that's so familiar you take it for granted because it happens almost every day of your life. You come home from work and walk through the front door. What's the first thing you and your family say to one another?

'What sort of day have you had? Tell me about your day.'

So you reply, 'Give me 20 minutes while I go upstairs and prepare a PowerPoint; because otherwise, you're never going to remember what I share with you.' Is that what you do? Of course it isn't. What *do* you do? You tell a story, like this:

'You won't believe what happened on the M5 this morning. There was a van on fire in the middle lane. Even the tarmac caught light. It was carnage!' Then it's your partner's turn:

'Everything was fine until I went down to the supermarket. It was so busy there was a queue to get into the car park. I got most of the things I wanted but they'd run out of cauliflowers. Can you believe a supermarket could run out of cauliflowers? When I got home, I thought I could relax but then the baby threw up on the carpet. I've had a dreadful day.'

Finally, it's the teenager's turn: 'You'll never guess what Dan did in chemistry today. You know what a clown Dan is. He dissolved a textbook in nitric acid. The chemistry teacher went ballistic! It was hilarious. Absolutely hilarious.'

Okay. *For a moment, close the book and recite those three stories before you open the book again.* Done that? Easy wasn't it? No visual aids, but I bet you remembered every sentence. So where did those statistics come from that say you won't remember unless you see it in pictures? Here's the point. When we're dealing with figures, that's true. When we're dealing with statistics, that's true. When we're dealing with facts, that's true. It's true because we don't relate to figures. Statistics are boring. But, since when was the purpose of a presentation to get someone to remember a load of statistics? That is never the aim of any presentation, is it? If it is, it shouldn't be.

Let's take another example. Imagine an army officer commanding a troop of soldiers in Afghanistan. They are being sent into situations which are extremely dangerous. Some of them will not come back alive; but it's his job to inspire them to risk their lives for a cause. If he can't do that without using PowerPoint, he shouldn't be leading them in the first place, should he? If he did deliver his battle speech to the troops and used PowerPoint, how inspiring would it be? You see, up to a point, it's true, a picture is worth a thousand words, but it's a picture about facts! Now facts may be relevant in a speech, but here's the point. Facts are not what inspire people. Facts are not what engage an audience. Facts are not what leave your audience hanging on your every word. Why? Because facts have no emotional content. On their own, facts are boring. Audiences engage with emotions.

The aim of a presentation may be one of the following:

- ▼ To educate you
- ▼ To persuade you to take action
- ▼ To persuade you to the speaker's point of view
- ▼ To convince you that the speaker is an authority on the subject
- ▼ To entertain you

While the presentation may *include* a statistic here and there to add credibility, the purpose of the presentation is *never* to get the audience to remember those figures. If that's all you succeed in doing, however effectively, what have you really achieved? Nothing.

The star of the show is you

Have you ever been to a pub with a friend and, somewhere in the background, there's a TV screen? There's a football match and there's breaking news – news of a tsunami in Japan. Where do your eyes go? Your friend is talking to you. You should be looking at your friend, concentrating on what he or she is sharing with you. But where do your eyes go? To the TV screen. It takes a real effort of will to avoid your eyes focusing on the TV. It's the same with a PowerPoint presentation. The first rule of any presentation is this:

Engage with your audience.
Make eye contact with them

So what do we do? We set up a massive screen for them to focus on and then we wonder why they're not relating to us! How daft is that?

The star of the show is **you**, not the screen. The most memorable thing about your talk should be you, not a set of slides. *Only Memorable is Good Enough.*

Tell a story

We're all natural-born story tellers. We always have been. Today, it's carnage on the M5. For our ancestors it was probably something even more exciting, like nearly being eaten by a sabretooth tiger! If we're naturally good at storytelling, why not play to our strengths? There's nothing quite like a story to really engage your audience – nothing that other people relate to better than a story. Why? Because it's happened to them; and because it's happened to them, they relate to it *emotionally*. It doesn't matter what the emotion is. It could be sharing something really funny ('you'll never guess what Dan did today') or it could be frustration ('it was carnage on the M5 today'). Include a story that your audience relates to emotionally. They know

Dan, or someone very like Dan. They've been stuck in a jam on the M5 themselves; they know what it's like.

There's another reason for using stories rather than statistics. Statistics can be challenged – 'Where did that figure come from? Is it reliable? I've seen figures from another source and they suggest the complete opposite of what you're claiming.' Even if your figures are accepted as accurate, your interpretation of them may be challenged. You may be accused of putting spin on your figures, or you may be accused of bias if your figures tell only part of the story. There may be someone in the audience who is more knowledgeable than you and who knows some figures that you have never seen. Now you're in trouble aren't you? By contrast, stories are fact. Stories are personal experience. As long as you bear the following tips in mind, they are much more difficult to challenge:

▼ They must be relevant to the point you are sharing with your audience.

▼ They must be stories that your audience is likely to relate to.

▼ They must include emotional content: amusement, frustration, anger.

Tell the story using a bit of drama. Don't be afraid to exaggerate as long as you're not blagging. There's a difference between exaggeration and blagging. We exaggerate for effect all the time: 'I nearly died!' 'There was blood all over the motorway!' 'I was wetting myself laughing!'

Everyone knows you did not nearly die, didn't wet yourself and that there wasn't blood all over the motorway; but phrases like these add colour to any story and that's what makes the story come alive. That's what makes the story memorable.

Am I saying that you should never do a PowerPoint presentation under any circumstances? No. Include PowerPoint under the following circumstances:

1. One of the purposes of your presentation is to prove that you are capable of producing a professional PowerPoint.
   For instance, as part of a job selection process.

2. If the presentation will suffer if you don't.

There may be others but I can't think of any. These are the only situations in which I would *ever* resort to using PowerPoint.

Structuring your presentation

The purpose

▼ Decide what the purpose of your talk is. Is it to educate, entertain or persuade?

▼ Be quite clear what outcome you're working towards, particularly if this requires the audience to act on something you shared with them.

Opening your presentation

Most speakers begin by introducing themselves: 'I'm Barry Jackson from BWJ Enterprise and I've been running my own business for several years now...' This is a turn off. I mean, who cares? Members of the audience are already beginning to yawn and you haven't even started! Your first move must be to **command the stage.** Come across as a speaker who has presence. There are several ways to do this. Here are a few of the best approaches. Notice that each is an immediate attention grabber.

▼ Begin with a story: 'On the way here, I was driving up the M5 when suddenly...'

▼ Tell them what you're going to say. Say it. Close by reminding them what they've been told.

▼ Use a relevant quote: 'Martin Luther King once said…'

▼ Ask them a rhetorical question. A rhetorical question does not require anyone to offer an answer. For instance: 'Have any of you ever arrived late for a really important appointment, because there was carnage on the motorway?'

▼ Ask a question that requires audience involvement:' Can you put up your hand if you've ever been late for an appointment because there was carnage on the motorway?' This requires the audience to do something, in this case, to put up their hands. Involving them avoids them being distracted. It's a great technique if you find that there are unexpected noises from outside, such as workmen drilling into the adjoining wall! If you're going to use this technique, make sure you invite an action which requires most of the audience to put up their hands. You can then invite them to look around at all the other people with raised hands. This is a great way to make everyone feel that they're all in the same boat and that you understand where they might be coming from.

▼ The big silence. This one takes nerve; but it's immensely powerful. It relies on the fact that the audience is expecting you to start speaking the moment you stand up. Nothing gets their attention more effectively than remaining completely silent and simply making eye contact with them. The trick is to watch their reactions closely. As long as you watch the body language, you will be able to discern the moment when they are about to tip over from dying to hear what you have to say, to a feeling of, 'come on, get on with it.' It's at that point that you begin speaking. It takes nerve because the silence seems three times longer to you than it does to your audience. Try it. It works.

The body of the talk

Whatever your subject, bear the following in mind:

▼ Speak with enthusiasm and passion. *Passion inspires.*

▼ Vary the tone and pitch of your voice as well as the pace at which you talk. If there's no variety in your voice, people will drift off. They may even fall asleep. You must avoid monotony When you're preparing your presentation, note where you're going to speed up or slow down. Give some thought to when it would be a good idea to raise or lower your voice.

▼ Match your voice and body language to the message you're delivering. If you want your audience to feel amused, smile at them; better still, laugh. If you want them to feel indignant, shout. Sound angry. Use gestures that emphasise what you're saying. For instance:
'There are three reasons why I believe this to be true.' (Hold up three fingers.)
'The impact of this on your business will be huge.' (Raise your voice on the word huge and make an expansive gesture with your arms.)
'We can ignore the effect because it's going to be tiny.' (Lower your voice on the word tiny and hold your thumb and forefinger close together to emphasise how tiny the effect will be.)

▼ Move with purpose. Most speakers make the mistake of either wandering all over the place, which is very distracting, or standing like a statue rooted to the spot. Don't move too much and when you do move, do so with purpose. For example, you want to make eye contact with different sections of your audience and it helps if you move to right and left. This does not mean pacing like a caged animal, though!

▼ Remember the power of three. I have no idea why this technique works. All I can tell you is that every professional speaker I've ever listened to uses it and it does work. It goes something like this. Let's say you want to make the point that story telling is an essential part of any good presentation. You could say that and no more. Or you could say the following: 'Stories are fun. Stories are relatable. Stories are your truth!' That's the power of three. Just as an exercise, read through this chapter again and see if you can spot one or two more examples that I deliberately threw in before I told you what technique I was using.

▼ Use humour. Some people are natural entertainers. If you fit into this category, don't be afraid to be funny. Audiences absolutely love people who make them laugh. It's almost impossible not to like someone who's entertaining. If you're a natural comedian, just make sure your talk doesn't become so funny that the central message is lost. If you're not naturally funny, don't try to be. There's nothing worse than attempted humour which doesn't come off! Whatever you do, avoid humour involving bad language or bad taste. There's no excuse for offending people. If you do, it's not just *this talk* that will be a disaster. Your whole reputation will be damaged.

The close

A strong close is as important as a powerful beginning – it's all too easy for a talk to just fade into nothing at the end. How you decide to close will depend on the purpose of the talk. If the purpose was to get the audience to act on what they've been told, invite them to do so. Make it quite clear what you're expecting them to do as a result of having listened to you. If it wasn't that kind of talk, a good technique might be to take the talk full circle by ending with the same quote or story that began the presentation. Another approach might be to remind the audience what you told them you were going tell them and that that's exactly what you just did.

General points

Here are a few general pointers to help you make excellent presentations:

▼ Be authentic. Be yourself. However impressed you may be with other speakers, it's a huge mistake to try to imitate someone else. You will be a shadow of your real self if you do. If you have an extrovert personality, do a bit of entertaining. Just make sure you don't get so carried away that you come across as flippant, that's all. If you are a more reserved personality, that's fine. As long as you come across as sincere, you will impress. You *will* be memorable.

▼ Tell jokes against yourself. While a speaker is meant to come across as the expert in the room, even experts mess up occasionally. All of us mess up from time to time and there's nothing that makes you less easy to relate to than coming across as a speaker who appears to be perfect. It's essential to come across as human. Don't be afraid to include the odd story against yourself.

▼ Don't restrict audience involvement to the beginning of the talk. Use the same techniques to involve them throughout your presentation, especially if it is for more than five minutes.

▼ This brings me to a very important point indeed: the need to stick to time. If you've been given five minutes, finish in five minutes. If you've been given 20 minutes, make sure it is 20 minutes. Nearly all speakers run way over their allocated time and there's no excuse for doing so. If the talk is more than five minutes long, (let's say 20 minutes) know where you should be in your talk at 5, 10 and 15 minutes. Then you can speed up or slow down a bit as the situation demands. Make sure there's a visible clock in the room. And remember that there may be other business following your talk; the audience wants to get on with it. Or your talk may be the final item, in which case people want to beat the traffic and get home. Running over time is bad planning and people resent speakers who do so.

▼ Should you use notes? No. Speak *without* using notes. I'm convinced that one of the reasons speakers are so keen on PowerPoint is because they can use their slides as crib sheets. Watch how much time they spend reading from their own PowerPoint slides and you'll see why I believe this. It's almost impossible to read from notes, including slides, and *really* engage with your audience at the same time. There are two ways you can avoid the use of notes. Find which one works for you. The first approach is to memorise your talk word for word. This may work for talks up to five minutes in length; but the longer the talk, the more difficult this becomes. In this case, memorise the key points from the talk and be prepared to ad lib the way you put across those points. Although I advise never using notes, it's a good idea to have prompt cards to hand. The reason for this is that most speakers' biggest fear is forgetting what comes next and going completely blank half way through. Having prompt cards to hand is a sensible form of back up. My experience is that, because this takes away the fear of going blank, the cards are hardly ever needed.

This chapter is perhaps the least heretical in the book. I say this because I have hardly ever seen a professional speaker, especially a motivational speaker, use PowerPoint. The most engaging speakers never do.

CHAPTER TEN

Leadership is NOT a Position

Never make the mistake of thinking that the time to lead is when you get a promotion; the time to lead is now. Whenever I ask a student who is a prefect or the captain of a sports team what led to her being selected for the role, the answer I almost always receive goes something like this:

'I have always been willing to take the lead.'

'I've never been afraid of accepting responsibility.'

'I've always been one to set the example to others.'

In other words, they were selected because they were comfortable taking the lead, even before they were formally offered a leadership position. Leadership is not about position. Leadership is an attitude of mind. So much so that a person who is not necessarily the team captain may, nevertheless, be the team's greatest source of inspiration. You can be that person long before you are offered an office with your name on the door!

Learning from Johnny

In this respect, I would like to talk about someone who has been a hero of mine for a long time. If I tell you that my favourite sport is rugby, it won't surprise you to know that his name is Johnny

Wilkinson. What may surprise you is the reason Johnny is one of my heroes. It's not because he's such an outstanding rugby player – although he is. It's not because I almost went demented when he put over that World Cup winning drop goal against Australia – although I did. It's because of the values that Johnny stands for on and off the pitch. You see, Johnny Wilkinson is the ultimate team player. If he started on the bench, you can see the morale of the team rising when he's brought on. His very presence on the field is an inspiration to every player around him. Johnny has rarely, if ever, captained the England side, yet he is a greater inspiration than many players who have.

I never really appreciated what his secret was until I heard him interviewed after that sensational Rugby World Cup final. After the more obvious questions like, 'How does it feel to score the winning drop goal in a World Cup final?' (to which there can be only one answer) the interviewer said to him, 'I suppose we ought to spare a thought for the losing Australian team. What must it be like in the Australian dressing room?'

'The atmosphere,' Johnny answered, 'will be awful.'

'I guess,' the interviewer continued, 'that you must, yourself, have been in that situation. You've given it everything, absolutely everything and still ended up on the losing side.'

'Every sportsperson has been there," Johnny answered. "Every sportsperson knows that feeling.'

'So, when that happens, how do you handle it?'

Johnny's answer tells you everything about the man, the values he holds dear and the values which define him as a person, not just as a rugby player. Here's what he said:

'The problem any sports team faces is that, on the day of a game, you have no influence over how your own teammates are going to perform, let alone how the opposition are going to perform. The only performance over which I have total control is my own performance. I owe it to myself and to my team colleagues to turn in the best performance of which I am capable. As long as I can walk off the pitch at the end of the game knowing that, by my own personal performance, I deserve to be on the winning side, I can handle just about any result.' No wonder Johnny is such an inspiration to every player on his team.

There are going to be times when you've given it everything and the result will still not be the result you were hoping for. There are times when you must accept yourself as a winner, no matter the outcome, especially when you can say that, by your own personal performance, you deserved to win.

Learning from Kirstie

Let's end with one last story. It's a true story, but the girl's name has been changed. Kirstie was a very competitive 11-year-old girl and a natural sprinter. In the school sports, she comfortably won the 100-metre race and qualified to represent her school at district level. She was now up against the fastest girls from all the other schools in the district. Did she win? You bet she did; and this qualified her to compete in the county championships, running against the fastest girls in the county. Do you think she was nervous? She was very nervous. Come on Kirstie, come on! Did she win? She did indeed! Yes!! Now she'd qualified to take part in the Scottish Junior Championships. If she won this event, she would be running for her country. As an added bonus, she was offered free training under Frank Dick, the British Olympic coach. Week after week, he worked on her running style, standing beside the track, stopwatch in hand, encouraging her as her times consistently improved. Come the day of the big race, do you think she was nervous? Kirstie was frightened to death. Come on Kirstie, come on! Did she win? Not this time.

Where did she finish? You really want to know? She finished last. The girl who didn't know what it was to be beaten over 100 metres had finished last.

Just beyond the finishing line, Frank was waiting for her. She was sobbing as she approached him. Frank said, 'Kirstie, you just ran the race of your life. I am so proud of you.'

She screamed at him, 'No I didn't. I was terrible. You're just saying that to make me feel better.'

'Kirstie,' Frank repeated, 'you just ran the race of your life.' Producing the stopwatch, he showed her the time, a personal best performance; the fastest 100 metres she'd ever run.

This is going to happen to you, too. You will turn in personal best performances and the outcome will not always be the outcome you hoped for. Remember, it's still the best performance of your life. Don't beat yourself up about it. Just as importantly, it's going to happen to members of your team and it's going to be up to you to show them that this was a personal best, that you're proud of them and that you have every reason to be proud of them no matter what their finishing position might be. I know there's a saying, especially in the commercial world, that second is nowhere. While I understand that point of view, it ignores the Kirsties of this world, the personal best performances, and the performances of team members whose personal contribution tells you they deserve to be on the winning side. As a leader, it's your responsibility to raise their morale at times like this and you will absolutely fail them if you concentrate only on outcomes and finishing positions. If it really is true that second is nowhere, what if you have 50 sales reps? Does that mean you have 49 losers in your team? As a leader you cannot afford to have your team think that way. You certainly can't afford to let them think that you value them only when they finish first. They probably gave it everything.

CHAPTER ELEVEN

Are People REALLY your Greatest Asset?

They ought to be. If they're not, you've got a problem. So where's the heresy here? Well let's run a few true stories past you so you understand what you might be up against:

A member of your staff calls in sick far more often than anyone else in the team. You haven't failed to notice that his sickness almost always coincides with a Champions' League game on the telly.

▼ A member of your team phones in sick. You visit his Facebook page and see pictures of him throwing up after a night of heavy drinking when he knew he had an early shift the next day. Not only this, he's boasting about how 'mullered' he was.

▼ A female member of your team is pregnant. She reports for duty but hardly ever does any work. When you challenge her she says, 'I can't do it because I'm expecting.' This is her response when asked to perform even the most undemanding task. You point out that other pregnant girls are managing without a problem. She eyeballs you and says, 'You know what I'll do if you make me do it and I have a miscarriage.'

There are employees out there whose standard answer to almost anything goes something like this:

'You can't prove it. You know what I'll say if...' There are employees out there who run rings around you, and always with the backing of the law behind them. They know their rights inside out and take full advantage of them. They are a pain in the backside. Others end up doing the work they ought to be doing and which they are being paid to do. Even their own colleagues despise them. These people are downright dishonest and deserve no sympathy whatsoever. This kind of situation, where you are dealing with a person with a damaging attitude, is very different to a situation where someone has simply made a mistake, however bad, and they desperately need your forgiveness. Equally, where they have given their all, things didn't work out, and they need to know you still value them.

Handling difficult employees

However compassionate you are, you are going to be faced with staff who are bone idle, dishonest or whose behaviour is so irresponsible that they jeopardize the profitability of the organization and the safety of people around them, and they don't even care. You would do anything to get rid of them. In fact, they deserve to be fired, but the law prevents you from getting rid of them.

It's as well to remind ourselves of a painful truth, a truth which John Maxwell put this way:

'You cannot make a commitment to uncommitted people and expect to receive commitment from them.'

Why am I telling you this? Two reasons really. Firstly, you have to be ready to know how to handle situations like this. Secondly, these people can be so infuriating that you can be provoked into doing something which appears to be perfectly fair but which infringes employment law. This is just what they're hoping you will do, because now they can take you to an industrial tribunal and sue you for compensation. It's just not fair. You're the good guy, remember.

How did this happen?

Here's what you **must** do. Share your frustration with your superiors. Even they may not be experts when it comes to employment law. Neither am I by the way; I don't know the answer to these people either. The only people qualified to advise you how to handle it are the people in the HR department and the company lawyers. If the company you work for is too small to have a legal or HR department, there are plenty of self-employed HR consultants who will provide advice. If there is a way of managing these dreadful people out, these are the people who know how it can be done while staying within the law. You must stay within the law. If you go outside the law, however unwittingly, it will backfire on you and you could end up facing disciplinary proceedings yourself, and that's definitely not fair! But take heart, staff like the ones described above are rather like criminals, they may get away with it for a while. It may seem that they have you over a barrel, for a while, but your time will come. They almost always overplay their hand eventually and then... Well then it's time to tear them limb from limb and say 'Gotcha!" because you've been waiting a very long time for this moment and it doesn't half feel good!

> *Look, I never said this was going to*
> *be a book about political correctness.*

CHAPTER TWELVE

The Ultimate Heresy: The Contract of Employment

So far, I've been merely heretical; now it's time to be outrageous. I'm going to make a suggestion that will make the hair of every HR manager in the country stand on end.

Let's consider the Contract of Employment. Yes, I know it's a legal necessity to have one. Without it, staff will have no idea what their responsibilities are or what you, their employer, are legally entitled to enforce. The Contract of Employment document details not only salary, holiday and pension entitlement, but responsibilities, notice of termination required, disciplinary and dismissal procedures as well as appeal and grievance procedures. While these must be clearly laid out for legal purposes, the wording of such a document is, by its very nature, threatening:

▼ These are your responsibilities. Implication: failure to achieve them may be construed as underperformance and appropriate action taken against you.

▼ Disciplinary and Dismissal: these are the situations in which *you agree* that we may take proceedings against you, *possibly leading to termination of your livelihood.*

▼ Appeal and Grievance: in return, we agree that, if we fail to follow the above procedure, *you may, in turn, threaten us* with legal action.

In other words: These are the rules by which we may engage in conflict. Sign here please!

Hang on a minute, isn't conflict something we want to avoid? Isn't it supposed to be bad for business, bad for morale, bad for just about everything?

Now ask yourself two vitally important questions:

1. Am I being unfair in what I just said?

2. Does this create trust, a feeling of being valued, a feeling that initiative is respected and that the taking of calculated risks is encouraged, and a feeling that mistakes are forgivable? Or does it create a mindset that says, 'I'd better be careful and watch my step, otherwise I could drop myself right in it!'

What effect does this stuff have on **motivation**? What effect does it have on **loyalty?** Is it the kind of language that fosters an attitude that says, *'I will give my all for you?'*

> *"Don't have a job description.*
> *Have a mission description."*
>
> Todd Skinner

Okay, suspend judgment for a moment. I want you to use your imagination and here's what I want you to imagine. A candidate has really impressed you at interview; so much so that you offer the job to him/her. The candidate accepts, but on condition that you read the following document. Here's what it says:

> *'With deepest joy I accept your kind offer to join your company. From this day forward, I pledge the following: all that I am I will gladly share with you and with everyone in the company. For better or for worse, through financial prosperity or crisis, when we are succeeding beyond our*

wildest dreams or we are in turmoil, whether we're proud of our achievements or facing disappointment, from the depth of my being, I will seek to be open and honest with you. I will honour your goals and do everything within my power to help you achieve them. Through the pressure of the present and the uncertainty of the future, I promise to be loyal to you. Many new responsibilities face me; and, as we begin together the great adventure of building this great enterprise, I can be counted on to do all that is expected of me and to prove myself worthy of the challenge that lies ahead of us. This is my pledge to you. This is my solemn word of honour.'

When you advertised the post, you invited applications from committed individuals. How do you feel about a candidate who is willing to offer this kind of commitment? Are you likely to have to take disciplinary action against someone with this strength of character and this attitude? Are you? Ever? But are you impressed; glad that this was the candidate you chose? Are you sceptical that he/she may not be serious? Are you feeling a little intimidated, knowing that if the candidate **is serious,** you're going to be asked to make a similar commitment to him or her. And, if you find that intimidating, wishing perhaps that you hadn't made the offer to this candidate after all, is it because that's not the kind of commitment you really want to make to your staff? Of course you believe in commitment, but you have to draw the line somewhere and that's going a bit far, right?

But suppose, just suppose, that instead of waiting for a candidate to come up with a contract like that, you took the initiative. Just suppose that, at the job interview, you handed each candidate a pledge like that and said, 'If you are offered the job, this is the kind of commitment we expect and this is the kind of commitment you can expect from us.' Let me tell you something: you would end up with the most committed, most loyal team you ever had in your life. You would end up with a team who would die for each other, and for you. Your corporate goal would no longer be a mere target for them; something to be appraised at the end-of-year salary review! It would become a cause for them. In their eyes, you would be no mere manager; you would be someone they looked up to. Their role model. Their hero.

Could you handle that?

CHAPTER THIRTEEN

Developing Your Active Listening Skills

We're just about at the end of the book. Maybe it's time to get away from heresy. I want the book to end on a high note, which is why I've left perhaps the most important tips in the whole book 'til last. When I was a teenager, my father once said to me, 'The art of being a good conversationalist is to be a good listener.' That sounded like good advice, but it left a few unanswered questions, such as these:

'What should I be listening for?'

'How do I know when I've heard it?'

'When I do hear it, what should be my next move?'

Become a fantastic conversationalist

During my years in business, it's been my experience that **nothing is more important to success than the ability to relate to, and to engage with, other people.** The techniques I'm about to share with you will prove invaluable when members of your team bring problems to you, or when you need to review performance which is falling short of what is expected of them, but you need to raise the subject in a non-threatening, non-manipulative way.

While these skills will prove invaluable in your future careers, you will also find that they will prove every bit as useful in your social lives, making new friends at university, avoiding conflict and impressing people you would like to impress such as tutors, parents and interviewers. One of the most rewarding things about developing your listening and questioning skills is that other people begin to regard you as a fantastic conversationalist, even when *they* did almost all the talking! The reason is simple: most people's favourite topic of conversation is themselves.

Let me share with you then, some of the techniques I have found most valuable – approaches you may never have had explained to you in quite these terms before.

Levels of engagement

When we respond to something another person just told us, we might convey any one of the following messages.

- ▼ I understand what you're saying, but I'm not interested.
- ▼ I understand what you're saying, but I haven't clue why you think that way.
- ▼ I understand how you're feeling, but I don't care.
- ▼ I understand how you're feeling, but I don't think you have any right to feel that way.
- ▼ I understand how you're feeling, but that's not how I would feel.

These are not very encouraging for the other person are they? They want our response to convey the following:

1. I understand what you're saying.

2. I understand why you're saying it.

3. I understand how you're feeling about it and why you would feel that way.

If any one of these is missing, we are not empathizing as well as we could.

There are several levels of engagement when we are talking with other people. There is the purely factual level: 'What are you doing over the bank holiday?' Next there's the motive behind the answer – the **what's in it for them** level: 'Why did you choose to go to Bournemouth?' Finally, there's the emotional level: 'Sounds as if you're in for a really *exciting* time.' It's at this level that you begin to really empathize with the other person because, now, you're *demonstrating* that you understand their feelings about whatever it is you're talking about.

What follows may sound complicated; but if you bear these points in mind as we go into more depth, it will help you realize which level you're at, which is really rather straightforward.

Strategies for conversation

The closed question

The simplest type of question is the **closed question, such as**, 'Did you have a good day today?' We call this a closed question because it can be answered with a straightforward yes or no. It's not a very exciting technique and it doesn't encourage the other person to share much more than a yes or a no. It can lead to a pretty boring exchange and will soon become irritating for the other person.

'Did you do such and such?'

'Yes'

'And did you do something else?'

'Yes'

'Could you have so and so?'

'No. I couldn't.'

There's a version of this type of questioning that can be threatening, even when that's not our intention. Let's say I were to ask you, 'Do you always clean your teeth every day?' Your answer is probably, 'nearly always.' It could be that you clean your teeth 364 days out of 365, but that's not quite always. The question puts you on the defensive. Another example might be, 'Do you always hand your homework in on time?' Questions which include absolute terms such as always or never sound like questions that are intended to catch you out. They sound manipulative and are best avoided. People get resentful if they feel they're being led into a trap!

The open question

A far better approach, because it encourages the other person to open up to you, is the **open question, such as,** 'What sort of day have you had?' You're already familiar with the fact that open questions begin with the words, what, why, which, when, who and how. Good though this approach is, even this type of questioning begins to sound like a cross-examination if you pursue it for too long. Any type of questioning can become a cross-examination if you're not careful. A good way to vary your approach is to encourage the other person to open up without using any form of question. "Tell me about your day" is not a question at all, but the other person will feel comfortable responding to it. You're giving permission for him or her to do just that – to tell you about their day.

Bridging techniques

Once the other person has begun opening up to you, you can move away from questioning by the use of what I call **bridging techniques.** There are literally hundreds of examples of these, including the following:

'Tell me more.'

'Really?'

'Surely not?'

The long pause

Once the other person is really into her stride, you don't even need to speak at all! In fact, you may do no more than nod your head. We'll say a bit more about body language in a minute. And don't forget the power of a **long pause**. Use this technique sparingly; it's a great approach when you sense that she just said something very significant, but you're not sure why. A pause will usually bring this out into the open; it's a way of saying go on without using the actual words. In fact it's a lot more powerful than if you did say the actual words. If you think it feels a bit awkward to do that, it does. That's why it works so well. People don't like long silences; but that's why we have to use this technique selectively and not too often.

The dropdown menu technique

One of the most important approaches to conversation is to use what I call the **dropdown menu** technique. When you click on an icon on your computer, you are often presented with a dropdown menu. Click on one of the options and you may be presented with another dropdown menu; and you may have to go down several levels before you find the option you're looking for. Conversation can be very like this. We start with a presenting statement such as, 'I'm going to Bournemouth.' It's okay as a starting point; but behind this statement there may be all sorts of hidden treasures or hidden emotions and, like the dropdown menu on a computer, the really interesting, really significant stuff may be several levels down. We're now going to look in more depth at how we can go deeper, but in ways which will be non-threatening. That's because the purpose of what we do next is to encourage the other person. If we fail to do this, she will clam up.

The either/or technique

We have already covered two of the dropdown approaches that you can use, namely open questions and bridging techniques. There are lots more though; and the ones we choose will depend on what we want to find out. One of the simplest is the **either/or technique.** For instance, 'You say you rarely hand your homework in on time. Is that because the work is hard and takes longer than you expect, *or is it because* homework gets in the way of things you would rather be doing and you just don't get round to it?' Another version of the same question might sound like this: 'When people tell me they have difficulty handing in homework on time, it usually means either A or B. Which is it for you?' There's another possibility, which is a very effective way of demonstrating that you understand where he's coming from: 'When I handed my homework in late, it was almost always because of A or B. Are either of those true for you? Maybe that was just me.'

Testing your own understanding

We've all made this mistake haven't we? Someone tells us something and we interpret it a particular way, because that's what *would be true* if it happened to us. Then we make an assumption which is quite wrong and the other person says, 'That's not what I meant at all,' which is a polite way of telling you that you don't understand. It feels very awkward when that happens, doesn't it? How can we avoid that happening? This is an easy one. We just have to remember to do it, that's all. It goes like this:

> *'Sounds to me as if ... Am I right about that?"*

> *'I'm getting the impression that ... Am I right about that?'*

> *'What I understand you to mean is X, Y and Z. Am I right about that?'*

You'll be surprised how often you will be spot on and this builds enormous trust and rapport with him. She's thinking, 'She understands me.' He's thinking, 'This guy knows where I'm coming from.' There's bonding going on between you, right? Even if you were wrong, he's going to tell you; and the mere fact that you asked *demonstrates* that you want to understand, *that you care.* For most people, that's the bottom line. You care.

Finding out what it means to him or her

Okay, so you have a piece of information; now let's pretend that you want to find out how important this is to the other person. There are lots of ways you can go about this.

The power of direct questioning

You could simply **ask a very direct question**: 'How important is this to you?' Being direct is rarely going to cause offence. Here's an example:

"I mustn't be late. I have to be in Bournemouth by 4 p.m. at the latest."

'By 4 p.m.? Why?'

(There are so many more subtle versions that I'm going to stick with a handful.)

'Why 4 p.m.?' *(Open question.)*

'What's important about 4 p.m.?" *(Open question.)*

'What will the consequences be if you don't make it by four?' *(Open question.)*

'Sounds as if you're going to be in real trouble then, if you don't make it. Am I right about that?' *(Testing your understanding of the situation.)*

'It's going to be *really upsetting* if you don't make it, isn't it?' *(Testing your understanding of how she might be feeling about the situation.)*

Notice that we've been using a dropdown menu approach and we've now drilled down to the emotional level – *how she's going to feel* if she fails to get to Bournemouth on time. If it turns out we're in a position to help her, it's going to mean a lot to her. In fact, it's going to make her day.

One of my favourite techniques for assessing how important something is to the other person is to use the score-out-of-10 approach. It's as simple as this: 'On a scale of 1 to 10, where 1 doesn't matter at all and 10 is catastrophic, how important is this to you?' You'll be amazed how often people will go on and on about how dreadful something is until you ask this question – and the answer turns out to be three! It's a great way of getting people to put a problem into its true perspective, and it avoids you wasting your time trying to help someone solve something that didn't matter in the first place! That's very frustrating.

Play the devil's advocate

Another very good way to assess the importance of what you're being told is to play the **devil's advocate** card. It sounds something like this: 'It would be great if you could get to Bournemouth by 4 p.m.; but if you didn't make it 'til 5 p.m., it wouldn't make a lot of difference really would it?' You'll be surprised how often she's going to agree with this statement! Aren't you glad you asked? If it's as important as she's making out, her response will probably be rather indignant, 'Won't make a difference? Of course it will make a difference. I'll miss my connection and there isn't another train until tomorrow morning.' Okay, now you know what you're dealing with.

My biggest fear

Another really powerful approach is to use **my biggest fear**. Let's say she's told you there's not another train until tomorrow; but she hasn't exactly spelled out the implications and you want to show that you understand the difficulty she might face. Here's what you say: 'In your position, my biggest fear would be that I might not make it before 4 p.m. Is that what you're afraid of?' **My biggest fear** can be used in all sorts of situations and we'll look at some more in a moment.

Getting buy in

One of the most frustrating things about other people is that they will tell you how upset they are about something; you offer a solution, *which they agree is a good idea,* and then they never act on it. They stay in a mess. They might even blame *you* for the fact that they're still in a mess. Why do people do this? There are several reasons:

1. It wasn't as serious a problem as they made out. Solving it was never all that important.

2. The solution will involve some sort of commitment on their part, a commitment they're not prepared to make. This is simply another version of point 1.

3. They really rather like their problem. It makes them the centre of attention. Other people feel sorry for them and all this will disappear if someone solves it for them!

4. The solution was your solution not theirs. It might work for you but they can't see it working for them.

As far as points 1 to 3 are concerned, **any of the above techniques will work**; that's why we use them. We want to help people all we can, but we can't help someone who doesn't want to be helped. Neither can we help people who are not prepared to do even the smallest thing to help themselves. If we try to do so, we end up feeling very frustrated and stressed out because they demand more and more of our attention, all to no purpose. Being helpful does not mean allowing ourselves to be manipulated. Don't allow people like this to put you on a guilt trip. It's their favourite tactic. Don't fall for it!

Helping them find their own solution

When someone brings her problem to us, we kind of fall into the trap of feeling that it's up to us to advise, to suggest something she might do.

'If I were you...'

'Here's what I would do...'

'I think what you ought to do is...'

Why? Because it would work for us, and because we want to feel that we're being ever so helpful! So it's a trap that's ever so easy to fall in to. If only we could get her to come up with a solution *of her own.* That's the key. If it's her solution, she's much more likely to act on it. Moreover, if you empowered her to come up with a solution of her own, she gets the credit. She did it herself rather than you doing it for her; and she won't half feel good about herself. Don't for one moment get the idea that this will mean no satisfaction for you. The greatest reward for a leader is helping others to run their own lives, and putting them back in control of their own destiny. You cannot solve problems *for* people, without taking control *away* from them. Can you see why people might resent you when all you were doing was trying to be helpful? It took me a very long time to work that one out. So, how are we going to put them back in control? As always, it's about questioning and listening.

'Okay, I see why that might be a problem to you. On a score of 1 to 10, how important is this to you?'

'Pretty important then. Why?'

'I'd be very upset if that happened to me. Is that how you feel?'

'Let's say there were an answer, I'm not saying there is, (never promise a solution) but if there were an answer, how would you feel about that?'

'I'm sure you've given a lot of thought to this; what ideas have you come up with so far?'

'And what happened when you tried that?'

Make the wrong assumption

Here's another technique. **Make the wrong assumption.** This is a particularly good approach when he's saying all the right things but you get the feeling he hasn't acted on any of them! What did your maths teacher say when you told him you had a problem with quadratic equations? (And you know he almost certainly never told his maths teacher there was a problem!)

> *'Tell me why you didn't. It sounds as if it might just work if you did.'*

He may have no ideas and we'll come to that in a moment. But let's say he has got some ideas. How are you going to encourage him? How are you going to help him evaluate whether the idea has a chance of working or not? You take him through an *imaginary process.*

> *'Let's pretend you were to do that. What's going to happen next?'*

> *'What will the next step be?'*

> *'If that were to happen, how would it make you feel?'*

More closed questions

If you're sure he's going to feel good, **a closed question** will be a very encouraging option here: *'If that were to happen, you're going to feel pretty good aren't you?'*

Suppose he hasn't got any ideas as to how he's going to solve the problem. In that case, it's perfectly okay to come up with some suggestions as long as you test the waters as you go. We've already seen what will happen if we dump our own solutions on him, even if he agrees that the idea was a good one.

> *'Here's an idea. This is what would work for me. I'd like you to tell me if you think it would work for you.'*

> *'Suppose you did this. How well would that work out for you?'*

> *'Imagine you were to do this. Tell me how well that would work for you.'*

"Let's pretend that you tried this. How do you think things would work out?"

Notice that, while you are now suggesting ideas, you're not telling him what he *should* do or *ought to* do. You avoid being patronizing. Sometimes, he will say something like, 'I'll give that a try.' Beware of that word try. It usually implies that he's not committed. If he was, he wouldn't say, 'I'm going to try.' He would say he's going to do it, and when (next Tuesday). That's what committed sounds like. There are two reasons people say they'll try:

1. They're not confident that they can do it.

2. They're saying what they think you want to hear.

Don't be afraid to challenge them if they use the word try.

'Maybe I'm wrong, but I sense that you're not convinced that this is going to work. What's worrying you?'

'I'm not sure you're convinced. Is there something else, something we haven't talked about yet?'

You could of course be more direct, couldn't you?

'I'll give that a try.'

'Try?' (Followed by a long pause.)

'I'll give that a try.'

'Meaning?' (Another long pause.)

Body language

I said I would include a few tips on how to use encouraging body language. There are ways in which you can convey that you're hanging on every word the other person is saying to you, without so much as opening your mouth. You *instinctively know* what these are.

- ▼ Maintain eye contact.
- ▼ Smile.
- ▼ Nod your head.
- ▼ Stroke your chin.

It's basic stuff, but you would be amazed how many people don't even get the basics right.

Summary

The depth is not in the questions you ask. The depth is in the process, the process of taking the other person deeper. The purpose is to understand not just what's being said, but what's behind what's being said, and the feelings that lie behind what's being said. We're looking to establish emotional empathy and we're looking for opportunities to encourage, encourage and encourage some more. In the words of Robin Sieger, 'The person who does not encourage you has forfeited the right to influence you.'

Never forget to encourage everyone around you. They may be people who are responsible to you; they may be people to whom you are responsible. As children, we thrive on encouragement and praise. So, I have A QUESTION FOR YOU. At what age do you think you outgrow that need? At what level of seniority does it no longer matter to you if no one ever praises you anymore? Is it when you become head teacher? Is it when you become a company director? Is it when you become a mum or a dad? The answer is that we never do. Everyone needs encouragement.

And finally

What you have just read has been about how to question and listen skilfully; how to engage and empathize. Now let's close with a few tips that will stand you in great stead when you find yourself in positions of authority. Positions of leadership.

None of your team will ever be perfect (neither will you)

This needn't be a problem. One of the things I always said to people who worked for me was this:

'If ever I think there's a way you could be a better member of my team, will it be okay for me to tell you what it is?' They're not going to say no, but if this is as far as I go, it's manipulative isn't it? So I always follows this with, 'Are you sure? How am I going to be certain that I never cause offence to you?' This is not a question they've ever been asked before, but I make sure they give me an answer because it's very important that I know. The next thing I say to them is, 'By the way. I'm not perfect either. If ever you can think of a way that I could be a better boss to you, I'm giving you permission to tell me.' They are invariably gobsmacked by this, but there have been many occasions on which I have been extremely grateful to members of my team for telling me that I just got something wrong – and what I need to do to put it right. The best time to introduce this technique is when the relationship is fresh, both of you want things to work out for the best and there are no problems. If you wait until there are problems, it's a lot more difficult to avoid recriminations!

Keep opinions to yourself

It's all too easy to get into arguments about things that really shouldn't matter. If you're going to get into a fight, make sure it's about something that does matter. You have to know what your values are. If you don't know what you stand for, you'll fall for anything. You need to know when it's time to nail your flag to the mast; but most things are not that important. It's best just to keep your big mouth shut about the bees in your bonnet. We all have them. Don't allow them to swarm all over other people!

Boundaries of confidentiality and taking sides

It may have happened to you already. You're a prefect and a Year 7 student says something critical about a teacher, with the clear expectation that you may be able to do something about it. How are you going to handle this? Where do the boundaries of confidentiality lie? You're going to run into exactly the same thing at work. Someone's partner ran off with someone else; can you keep that confidential? Someone tells you he's gay; can you keep that confidential? Someone confesses to you that she fiddled her expenses; can you keep that confidential? As soon as there are people responsible to you, it's only a matter of time before this happens. You need to know what the company policy is. Never allow yourself to be compromised by not knowing. Ask *your* boss; and if you change companies, don't assume that every company is the same.

What if people complain about your boss's behaviour? This is not too difficult to handle until you find yourself in a position where you agree that they have a point. You find her difficult as well! The trick is to be on your colleague's side without *taking* sides. Never take sides. The best way to sidestep an issue like this is to ask the following question:

'I understand how you feel, but why are you telling me this?'

Whatever you do, avoid gossip. Gossip is extremely damaging and may well be untrue. A friend of mine, we'll call him Paul because that's his name, has a fantastic way of stopping gossip dead in its tracks. Whenever someone goes off on one about a work colleague, Paul simply says this:

'Really. And she speaks so highly of you.'

*I think that's a good note on which to
end a chapter, don't you?*

CHAPTER FOURTEEN

The Heretic Leader's Checklist

How do your leaders, and you yourself, measure up? How consistently do you apply the *Rule of Three* to members of your team? If they are themselves aspiring leaders, how consistently do they apply the Rule of Three to the people for whose welfare they are responsible?

The Rule of Three

So, what is the Rule of Three? The number of things that add up to respect and love for your people is large and can become confusing. Let's try and keep it simple shall we? I'm going to challenge you with a question. I have used this challenge many times and, so far, no one has been able to add to the list of three. No one has ever been able to make it the rule of four or more.

Think for a moment of something you have done that you were proud of. Have you got an example? I suggest to you that if it was something you were proud of it involved either an act of **courage** or an act of **compassion** or a **sense of humour.** Any other words you can think of, and I concede that there are a lot of them, come under one of those three headings. Now think of a situation in which you acted in a way that left you less than proud of yourself, maybe even ashamed of the way you behaved. In this case, I almost guarantee that it was because you wimped out of something you should have had the courage to face up to, or you were unkind, or you made an unhappy situation even worse by going on about how awful it was, rather than encouraging the other person to see the humour in it. Just about every challenge you have ever faced, or will ever face, can best be tackled using one of those three qualities courage, compassion or sense of humour (or a combination of the three). I challenge you to think of any situation that will not be improved by bringing one of those three to bear on it.

As leaders, we have to role model these three qualities and encourage others to do the same. A checklist of just three is pretty manageable isn't it? So, whenever you know you did really well, take a moment to review which of these three (or a combination of them) was the secret of your success. And if you messed up (you will), take a moment to consider which rule you violated and which of the three would have served you best. Add to the list if you can; but I bet you can't.

Our Team

In this team, I am a somebody

In this team, I am everyone else's hero

In this team, I can make a difference

We are a team of equals

In this team, everyone is on my side

In this team, everyone is my brother or my sister

*In this team, no one ever faces any kind of
trouble alone*

This is a fun team to belong to

This team brings out the greatness that is within me

*This team brings out the sleeping giant that is
inside me*

Belonging to this team is an inspiration to me.

**Here's a suggestion. How about having framed copies of this
on the wall of your office as an inspiring reminder to you and
your team? I do.**

Further Reading

As a leader, you must never stop learning how to become better at leading. You've heard the expressions, 'You can't teach an old dog new tricks' and 'A leopard cannot change his spots.' Leaders cannot afford that kind of wayward thinking. However good you become at anything, can you imagine ever wanting to reach the stage where you're the best you you're ever going to be? Heaven help us, you might as well be dead!

> *'You cannot work too hard on improving yourself as a person.'*
>
> **Fred Harteis.**

There are three ways in which you can get better and better and better. Here they are,

- ▼ Read books on your subject, especially leadership and understanding people.

- ▼ Model yourself on people who are wiser and more experienced than you are. These people will not always be older than you are.

- ▼ Learn from your own experiences. These will include experiences that you, and only you, have had. Such experiences will enable you to develop a wisdom that is all your own.

The following books have been an inspiration and a source of learning for me.

The Right to Lead: A study in Character and Courage by John Maxwell

The 21 Indispensable Qualities of a Leader: Becoming the Person Others Will Want to Follow also by John Maxwell.

John Maxwell is an acknowledged world authority on the subject of leadership. Any book by John Maxwell is a treasure trove of wisdom.

Hit the Ground Kneeling by Stephen Cottrell. This book appeals to me because it looks at leadership from a Christian standpoint with regular Bible references. Even if you're not a Christian, however, the principles outlined in this wonderful little volume are timeless.

Managing from the Heart by Hyler Bracey, Jack Rosenblum, Aubrey Sandford and Roy Trueblood.

Leadership and the One Minute Manager and *The Power of Ethical Management* by Kenneth Blanchard and others. Anything by Kenneth Blanchard is brief, to the point and can be read in not much more than an hour.

The 17 Essential Qualities of a Team Player by John Maxwell.

Who Do You Think You Are Anyway? by Robert A. Rohm, PhD and E. Chris Carey. A wonderful book explaining how our personalities shape our views of the world, and even our values, and how we can adapt our approach to one another so we protect our egos and each other's.

The Power of Meeting New People by Debra Fine

Listening for Success by Steve Shapiro.

Beyond the Summit by Todd Skinner.

Difficult Conversations by Clive Lewis

Resolving Workplace Conflict by Clive Lewis.

Acknowledgements

During the course of my career, many people have been inspirational role models to me. During my days as a young, very green, and at times extremely naïve sales rep I worked for a company called Delandale Laboratories. I benefitted enormously from the patience and constant encouragement I received from two senior managers in particular. Keith Fanthorpe and Paul Balmer role-modelled dynamic, inspirational yet compassionate leadership. It was a great sadness to me when Delandale was taken over and our team was split up; but our friendship endures. During my time with Delandale I was also privileged to meet members of the medical profession whose professionalism I admired enormously. Among these I count Professor Neil Johnson as another source of inspiration throughout my career.

When I decided that the pharmaceutical industry could manage perfectly well without me and set up my own coaching business there were new skills I felt I should acquire. Having chosen personality profiling as an area that particularly fascinated me, I discovered Dr Robert Rohm and his Personality Insights team. I chose Dr Rohm because he was the finest coach I could find anywhere in the world in this speciality. This meant a visit to Atlanta, Georgia, where Dr Rohm is based. He and his team made me, the only Brit on the course, extremely welcome. The regular contact I maintain with the Personality Insights team makes me feel like one of the family.

Shortly after my visit to Atlanta, I was privileged to attend training in London with the great Les Brown. Les rated in the top five motivational speakers in the world. It was while having lunch with Les that he suggested I join the Toastmasters International speakers' club. The friends I have made in my local Cheltenham branch are too many to be named individually, but I cannot omit mentioning John and Maria Evans, both of whom have been a particular inspiration to me and from whom I have learned so much about public speaking.

Membership of Toastmasters led me to join the Professional Speakers Association (PSA); my development as a professional speaker has taken another enormous leap forward as a result of the encouragement I have received from David Hyner (my personal mentor), Peter Roper and Graham Jones (former presidents), Lesley Matile and Angie Egan. It was they who, between them, persuaded me that writing a book was a good idea. I've always wanted to write a book.

On the subject of the book, 'giving birth' to it was down to the talents of Mindy Gibbins Klein (also from the PSA.) while Al Hidden has done a first-rate job as copy-editor of the original manuscript.

When I was creating my CD training program, entitled *Only Memorable is Good Enough,* I had the pleasure of working with Andrew Lansley at the Gloscat Studios in Cheltenham. Andy, who shares my love of Bavarian dark beer, was great fun to work with and showed great patience putting together all five hours of it. My thanks also go to former deputy head teacher David Butler, who contributed one of the tracks, and Kath Johnson who provided the voice-overs.

During my development as a salesperson, I was fortunate to meet Nigel Dunand and Mark Wormald from the Sandler Sales Institute.

It was Nigel and Mark who shared with me the fact that almost everything that most people think selling is about is wrong. Their courses developed my questioning and listening skills to a level I wouldn't have believed possible. The chapter on this subject has been inspired by the principles I learned through Sandler training.

When you first start out in business, you begin with no customers and no reputation. Whatever level of success you may reach eventually, that success must necessarily be built on the willingness of your very first customers to trust you before you have built that reputation. In this respect I will forever be grateful for the trust that the following pioneer teachers have placed in me:

> Stuart Langworthy and Richard Giddy, Brockworth Enterprise School, Gloucester.
>
> Raymond Friel (Head Teacher) and Martin Gailey, St.Gregory's Catholic College, Bath.
>
> Peggy Farrington (Head Teacher) and Jo Postlethwaite, Hanham High School, Bristol.
>
> John Lewis, St.Edward's Private School, Cheltenham.
>
> Rob Wallace, John Kyrle School, Ross on Wye, Herefordshire.
>
> Eileen Stead, Business Manager, King Charles I School, Kidderminster.
>
> James McCormick, Dame Elizabeth Cadbury School, Birmingham
>
> Terry Law, King Edward VI, Camp Hill School for Boys, Birmingham.

The list would be incomplete if I were not to mention Heather Lee and Kath Johnson from Gloucestershire Education Business Partnership and David Firmin's team from the Bristol EBP., all of whom were instrumental in introducing me to the above schools in the first place.

Finally, I just have to pay tribute to my family. I guess every father wants to be an inspiration to his own children, but nothing can give a father a deeper sense of pride than to see his two sons develop into young men who become his inspiration. I count Chris and Barney among my best friends and nothing beats having a beer or a curry together, sitting side by side at a Twickenham rugby game or a Gloucester game at Kingsholm. And what of Jenny, my wife? Jenny has been the foundation of every success I have ever had and my strength when things have been hard. Depending on your point of view, giving up a well-paid secure job to set up your own business when the economy is heading into deep recession might be described as courageous or just plain madness. It's even harder for your partner to watch you using up (sometimes squandering) hard-earned equity that might have provided for a secure retirement on a new venture that's not guaranteed to succeed. It takes a very special partner to offer unconditional support for such a venture, especially when she's never been interested in business and counts herself as politically left of Tony Benn. If ever there's an example of opposites being the magic ingredients of a devoted partnership it's me and my Jen. I love her as much as the day we first met – a whole lot more really. The day we first met, nothing much happened at all; but what do you expect outside Dorking Library?

About the Author

Barry Jackson obtained an honours degree in microbiology at the University of Reading in 1971. He worked in sales and marketing for a number of pharmaceutical companies over a period of 34 years. During this time, he fulfilled roles as area sales manager, key accounts manager and national product specialist. His time in the pharmaceutical industry involved working with some of the UK's top medical opinion leaders in the fields of psychiatry, gynaecology, cardiology, urology and microbiology. Barry also represented his employers at national and international medical symposia.

Since setting up his own company (BWJ Enterprise), Barry has become a fully qualified personality profiler, training under world-famous coach, Dr Robert Rohm. He is a member of the Professional Speakers' Association (Birmingham Chapter), The Global Speakers' Federation and the Toastmasters International speakers' club (Cheltenham Branch).

In addition to his experience in commerce, Barry was a member of the leadership team of the telephone Samaritans and has shared his leadership insights with children as young as seven, with teenagers and as father to his two sons (now in leadership roles in their own right). **Barry refuses to endorse anything that hasn't worked for him personally, merely because it's in vogue!** He enjoys sharing his experiences and training the principles he has learned with all aspiring leaders, but especially young people.

Barry has been married to Jenny for 34 years and runs his business from his home in Churchdown, Gloucestershire.

For training requests or speaking engagements, Barry may be contacted as follows:

www.bwjenterprise.co.uk

bwjenterprise@btinternet.com

07795 288 490

Lightning Source UK Ltd.
Milton Keynes UK
UKOW030621190712

196224UK00004B/13/P